PARAM VIR VIKRAM BATRA

THE SHER SHAH OF KARGIL

A father remembers

PARAM VIR VIKRAM BATRA
THE SHER SHAH OF KARGIL

A father remembers

GL BATRA

First published in India 2016

Times Group Books
A division of
Bennett, Coleman & Co. Ltd.
The Times of India, 10 Daryaganj, New Delhi-110002
Phone: 011-39843333, Email: tgb@timesgroup.in

PARAM VIR VIKRAM BATRA: THE SHER SHAH OF KARGIL

Cover caption: Vikram in action at Point 5140

Cover Image: (Top) Gettyimages

ISBN 978-93-84038-97-7

Price: ₹399

Printed at: Nutech Print Services - India

In loving memory of my son Capt. Vikram Batra, PVC,
the great son of the motherland.

Foreword

My father had served in Maharaja Hari Singh's state forces of J&K. These were subsequently merged en-bloc into the Indian army - the only princely state force that retained its own distinctive identity as a regiment. These state forces boasted of war heroes like Gen. Zorawar Singh, Gen. Baj Singh, Col Basti Ram and Brig. Rajinder Singh MVC - the man who actually saved Srinagar in 1947. My elder brother, Capt. SR Bakshi, joined this regiment in 1963 and was martyred in the 1965 war. I personally commanded 6.JAK Rifles in major skirmishes in Kargil in 1990-91. Capt. Vikrarn Batra was commissioned into the famous 13th Battalion of the JAK Rifles on 6 December 1997. Just two years later, diis battalion was pitchforked into die most intense fighting in J&K. The battalion fought very major actions in the Tololing sector, which proved to be die turning point of the entire -war. From then onwards defeat [turned] into victory. Point 5140 was the most dominating peak in this entire sector. After Raj. Rifles had taken Tololing, Vikram and his boys were ordered to capture the formidable Point 5140 in an amazing night assault. Vikram and his men scaled this Eiffel Tower-like peak from the most unexpected directiim. After a bitter hand-to-hand fight, they cleared this strategic feature. Vikram's exultant victory cry *Yeh dil maange more* (my heart yearns for more victories) infused enthusiasm among one and all. Barkha Dutt, the renowned journalist, made it ring out across the globe and Vikram became the iconic young face of the Kargil War. Thai by itself was an adequate achievement for any battalion. However, 13 JAK Rifles, however, was regrouped and launched into another fierce attack. Vikram was then down with fever bul insisted enjoining the attack on Point 4875, one of the most formidable and well-defended enemy posts. The unit took heavy casualties and was pinned down. Sensing the criticality of the situation, Vikram volunteered to lead the assault himself. He led his men up ihe that vertical cliff and got into a desperate hand-Ki-hiuid fight with Ihe Pakistanis. He himself killed five enemy Holdirra, Seeing him fight like a tiger, his men surged forth and cleared the whole feature. The enemy camp fled in panic and many of his soldiers fell to their death. Vikram died while putting one of his wounded soldiers to safety – a soul-stirring example of sacrificial altruism in the battefield. Capt. Vikram Batra was posthumously awarded the Param Vir Chakra, die highest gallantry award tor supreme courage and valour in the face of the enemy.

My family was fortunate to record this tale of great heroism in the form of an Indian War Comic in 2008. My son Adilya had started this series on the lives and actions of our PVC and AC winners. We were blessed to meet and interact with ihe brave Balm family and share their pain. I am glad today we have an occasion to share the glory that their earned for our regiment and the country, I am delighted to see this book by the father and family of one of India's bravest of the brave. I am certain that act of recording it all for posterity would have served in part to mitigate ihe pain of losing a young son. Vikram has entered the heaven of our war heroes - that Valhalla of the bravest of our brave. Interestingly, 13 JAK Rifles has to its credit not one but two PVGs in die Kargil conflict. It remains an unprecedented feat in the annals of our military history.

Message

It gives me a sense of great pride and elation to write about 'Sher Shah', one of the finest officers 1 had the privilege of serving with. No words are enough to describe the feat 'Vikram has achieved.

There are very few people in the world who, within a short span of life, leave an indelible mark in the history by their courage and valour. Vikram Batra is one such name that has been immortalized in the annals of the Indian history and has today become synonymous for courage, fortitude and never-say-die attitude in every Indian household.

Vikram, after commissioning in December 1997 from IMA, Dehradun, joined the 'Bravest of the Brave' family at Sopore, J&K. Endeared with great motivation and indefatigable energy, he soon earned his spurs in the battalion overcoming challenges through his determination, dedication and diligence. Vikram was a man of great courage and soaring spirit who never looked away from taking a challenge.

I am reminded of the incident when we were planning for the assault on Point 5140. 'Vikram was the 'D' Company Commander who was tasked to capture the feature. As we came out of our makeshift operation room, I asked Vikram as to what would be the 'success signal' after the capture, to which he replied *Yeh dil maange more.* I was little startled by his choice of a non-military 'success signal', to which he replied that after capturing the bunkers on Point 5140, he would be looking for some more bunkers to capture. I did not give it much thought at that time, but when Point 5140 was actually captured and he gave me the 'success signal', the phrase became so popular that it became the tagline of Army operations in Kargil.

Capt. Vikram Batra's courage, valour and inspiring leadership during the Kargil War of June 1999 during the capture of Point 5140 and, subsequently, Point 4875 have become part of folklore today and continue to inspire all of us and our future generations. He was not only brave but also had a heart full of compassion and care for his subordinates. In one of his interviews to the media, he mentioned that after the war he wanted to do something for the welfare of the families of the jawans who had made the supreme sacrifice during the war. It is an irony that when (he interview was aired on television on 07 July 1999, Capt. Vikram Batra had himself made the supreme sacrifice while capturing Point 4875.

I must extend my sincere gratitude and compliments to Mr GL Batra for painstakingly writing this book and giving us an insight into the life of Vikram, the face of the Indian Army during the Kargil War. This book takes you through the transformation of a young boy who ditched a high-paying Merchant Navy job to join the Indian Army and who, at a tender age of 24 with just 19 months of service, attained martyrdom upholding the highest traditions of Indian Army, which would serve as an inspiration for the generations to come.

– Maj. Gen. YK Joshi, AVSM, SM, VrC

Message

It is my proud privilege to write a note of tribute on Vikram Batra, a young boy from Palampur, who became an example of courage, duty and sacrifice in the Kargil War. I recall his motivation, commitment to task and affable nature, which endeared him to anyone who came into his contact. No commander could have asked for a more courageous lot of young officers like Vikram and his men.

Vikram's battalion, 13 JAK Rifles, was deployed in Sopore, while 8 Mountain Division was in the Valley in its counter-insurgency role. They were earmarked to move to Shahjahanpur (Uttar Pradesh) for their peace/family tenure. But fate had a different future chalked out for the unit a future that brought them immense glory in Kargil and won them laurels and awards which became the envy of any unit.

Vikram was part of this fine outfit which got inducted into the Kargil War as part of my Division. The war in Kargil was fought in the world's most inhospitable terrain and in severe weather conditions. Vikram was an example of dedication for his battalion. He was confident, with a charming personality and had an excellent quality of a leader. He was dedicated to his unit, his command, the task in hand and strived to achieve success and victory at all costs.

This is a book written by a proud father spanning his son's short but very distinguished life – a life that will be written in golden letters in the annals of Indian military history. It is a tribute to our young officers like Vikram who displayed courage and fortitude much beyond the call of military duty, sacrificing in the process their lives.

While reading the book, there is a very noticeable trait of the closeness of the family to each other. From childhood, Vikram was brought up with wonderful family values, which manifested in the love and respect he had for his parents and his unit and finally for the battlefield, bringing glory for himself and pride to his unit and family.

Vikram's bravery in the battles at Point 5140 and Point 4875 have become a part of folklore. Despite heavy odds, and in the most difficult terrains and under severe weather conditions, the unachievable was achieved by Vikram and his gallant command. His felicitation with Param Vir Chakra was most befitting and fully deserved. While he achieved martyrdom, he has left a legacy for thc younger generation, and I do hope they get adequately motivated to emulate his example.

– Lt Gen. Mohindcr Pun (Retd)

Message

I had the privilege to command the brigade that was actively involved in Operation Vijay in Drass in 1999 when I met Vikram for the first time as one of the company commanders of 13 JAK Rifles.

The elan, grit and zeal that Vikram possessed was clearly evident from the time I first met him. I was fully confident that with young lenders like Vikram Batra, 13 JAK Rifles was going to achieve wonders in the difficult limes ahead in whatever tasks assigned to them.

The first one to prove this was Vikram Batra, who led from the front to capture Point 5140, the first success of 13 JAK Rifles. The hunger for victory and the leadership skills displayed by him knew no bounds. The phrase coined by him, *Yeh dil maange more,* was most appropriate. His exceptional leadership qualities and fearlessness changed the outlook of the men he commanded. During the assault on Point 4875, Vikram, a valiant soldier, which he proved to be, charged the enemy bunker unmindful of his safety to achieve his goal in life. [He was] a man of insurmountable resolve and nerves of steel who laid down his life for the nation. The memory of Vikram remains etched in our hearts and the nation for times to come and shall always inspire the coming generations.

Contents

Author's Note

India, a land of diverse cultures, civilizations and a history older than one can imagine, has stood testimony to times, centuries and eras. It is the beholder of a past that has witnessed innumerable tragedies, victories and battles.

The country has integrated itself irrespective of the borders, enemies and threats. The soldiers who willingly lay down their lives for the safety and security of this great nation are the real heroes we owe our history to.

We must always remember that it is for our present that they have sacrificed their future. Their supreme sacrifice, integrity and valour must not go in vain. We must, at all times, attempt to make our nation worthwhile of their patriotism. The dignity and honour of our defence services and our selfless soldiers must always be our first priority. It is from these bravehearts we learn that duty comes first. Performing a duty wholeheartedly, without prejudice and bias, is in itself a form of worship to the nation.

Without our soldiers, the state of our country is unimaginable. Our country would be just another unprotected piece of land on the world map. A true spiritualist is always a true patriot and a true patriot is always a spiritualist.

It is with this aim of inspiring and encouraging our youth to follow a self-righteous path that I write this book. The citizens of our country must, in all their actions, keep national conscience and patriotic fervour alive. We Indians should be proud of our

Acknowledgements

I am grateful to Shyam Kumariji, who inspired me to write this book and for her tribute to my son VIkram Batra. A special thanks to Gaurav Sawant, author of *Dateline Kargil,* and Srinjoy Chowdhury, author of *Despatches From Kargil,* the two defence correspondents who visited the war zones at the time of Kargil War, in 1999. I have referred to their books extensively for accuracy and authenticity.

A special thanks to Gen. VP Malik (Chief of the Army Staff), Retd, who has encouraged us with his words on Capt. Vikram Batra.

I am also grateful to Maj. Gen. YKJoshi, Vikram's battalion commander during the period of Kargil War, for his memoirs and glorifications of Capt. Vikram Batra.

I am grateful to Ms Barkha Dutt for allowing me to borrow a note from her book, *This Unquiet Land: Stories from India's Fault Lines* and for writing her memories and gratification for Vikram Batra.

I am also grateful to Maj. Gen. lan Cardozo for being kind enough to allow me to borrow a note from his book *Param Vir: Our Heroes in Battle.*

I am particularly thankful to Lt Gen. Mohinder Puri (Retd) and Lt Gen. Amar Aul (Retd) for writing a message for the book.

I am thankful to Maj. Gen. (Dr) GD Bakshi (Retd) for providing the foreword.

I am also thankful to Pranab Punj and Rashmi Kaimal for the two poems that they have contributed for the book.

I would like to extend my sincere thanks to my wife Kamal Kanta Batra, who helped me to collect all the relevant material for this book and offered me endless cups of tea while I toiled over the manuscript. She also helped me in carrying out the corrections and improving the manuscript.

I am thankful to my son Vishal Batra, for getting the manuscript transformed into a soft copy and also letting me include his recollections of Vikram in the book.

Thanks to my daughters Seema and Neetu, who continued to inspire me to write the biography of their loving brother.

I am also grateful to Mr Inder Sharma, Chairman, Select Citywalk, for showcasing the book on the occasion of Kargil Vijay Diwas (26 July).

I would also like to acknowledge the contribution of Lt Col Hardeep Sandhu, Vikram's dear friend, also fondly called Nippy.

Last, but not the least, I am thankful to all my friends and well-wishers who encouraged me to write an ode to the great son of the nation.

What you believe about religion, philosophy, science, people, things — all these beliefs colour your life. But what you believe about yourself is most important of all, because you can never be anyone else but yourself only, and what you believe about everything else is closely related to what you believe about yourself.

— An excerpt from the diary of Capt. Vikram Batra

A FIGHTER IS BORN

**If death comes to me before I prove my blood.
I will kill it.**

Vikram was born on 9 September 1974 in a small town in Palampur, Himachal Pradesh. He was the elder of my twin sons; the younger one is Vishal.

He was the third child after two daughters, Seema and Nutan. Being a staunch believer of Lord Rama, my wife, Kamal Kanta, named the twin sons after the two heroic sons of Lord Rama — Luv and Kush.

Bonded from birth: The two toddlers Vikram and Vishal

Twin power: The brothers, Vishal and Vikram, shared a special bond from birth

Vikram (Luv) and Vishal (Kush) were identical twins in every respect, be it personalities, beliefs or mannerisms. My wife and I being academicians, Vikram got his primary education from his mother. Later, he was admitted to D.A.V School at Palampur, where he studied up to middle school. Thereafter, he did his plus two from Central School, Palampur.

Being a diehard patriot, every night 1 spoke to my sons, Vikram and Vishal, about our country's pride and valour. Vikram grew up listening to the stories of our struggles, revolutions and the Indian uprising. Vikram would over and over hear stories of Bhagat Singh, Chandra Shekhar Azad, Maharana Pratap, Guru Gobind Singh and Chhatrapati Shivaji.

These stories left an indelible imprint on his tender mind. They made him a strong and courageous person. He realized at a very young age that he must follow in the footsteps of his childhood heroes.

Even as a child, Vikram thought it to be his duty to help anyone

Gearing for life: Vikram and Vishal dressed for their first day at school

in need. His mother recalls how once he easily killed a poisonous snake as she watched paralysed with fear. Always a brave and fearless child, Vikram, during his school days on his way back, saved a girl from falling out of the school bus. She was standing right next to the door, which was not shut properly. Without thinking; twice, Vikram jumped after her and saved her from any serious injury. He took her to a nearby hospital for medical care. The cheerful and happy child then recounted the story to everyone matter-of-factly.

Vikram and Vishal with their trophies that they won in various school tournaments

Young Vikram: A child with a sunny disposition and a versatile personality

Born with an indommable spirit of adventure, Vikram was the best skater of Palampur Skating Club during his school days He was a green belt in karate and had even attended a national-level camp m Manali. Vikram even managed to learn squash from a friend at the local army camp. Often, Vikram and his friends would go on excursions to the Dhauladhar Hills in Himachal Pradesh in biting cold.

Vikram was a versatile child. Gifted with exemplary oratory skills, he was even selected to represent his school at the national level during the Youth Parliamentary competitions at Delhi.

He was academically brilliant and brought laurels to his school and college. Vikram represented his school and college in table tennis, karate and other such games. Both Vikram and Vishal were great sports enthusiasts, playing everything from cricket, table tennis, lawn tennis, squash and roller skating. There was hardly a day when they didn't spend two hours playing ping pong or taking to the lawns at the army cantonment for some lawn tennis or hammering the ball at the squash court. It was table tennis that made them the icons of Palampur. The Rotary Club of Palampur had even honoured both the brothers for their performance. They would defeat much elder

Raising his sights high: Vikram receiving a trophy for winning a tournament in school

members of the club. Vikram and Vishal went on to represent their school at All India KVS Nationals in 1990.

Even as a young boy, Vikram had shown signs of leadership qualities. His friends and teachers were extremely fond of him. He had a certain power to influence people and was an all-rounder. During a class strike in school, his principal approached Vikram to call off the strike. He was able to persuade the students for an amicable settlement and ensured that no classes were further disrupted.

Vikram 's dedication towards studies and an overall development and his supreme sacrifice for the nation in such a short span of life reminds me of a quote from his diary:

I have no 'stop' word in my dictionary,
I have to work and walk through dark, thorny streets,
Light and pleasure will themselves look for me.

COLLEGE DAYS

If you wish to reach the highest begin at the lowest

The school life ended on a high note for Vikram and Vishal as they had scored 82 per cent marks in the boards. The next mission was to get admission in a good college in a bigger city. D.A.V College Chandigarh was their first preference. Both the brothers were anxious as they would be staying away from home, in a hostel, for the first time. Both Vikram and Vishal opted for BSc Medical Sciences and got a hostel inside the college campus. Being twins gained them popularity within the college and hostel. Always

Fun and studies in equal measure: Vikram and Vishal on a picnic with their friends

Starstruck Vikram's room, with a poster of the iconic Marilyn Monroe

a go-getter, Vikram 'lived life king size'. He managed a great balance between studies and extra-curricular activities. Vikram always used to be among the top ten rankers of his class.

Ever outgoing and friendly person, Vikram had a wide circle of friends in college and in the hostel. Boys around him liked his joyous nature and happy temperament. He was also very friendly with the hostel mess boys. He would often lend them starstruck: Vikram's room, with a his motorbike and, in turn, the mess boys would provide him with lunch and tiffin even at odd hours.

Once I went to his hostel to meet him at 4 p.m. He immediately served me a plate of noodles with omelette spread over it and a cup of tea. Startled, I asked him how did he manage the lunch during mess off hours and he told me about his friendship with the mess boys. I was really touched by his behaviour.

On another occassion, Vikram had managed to secure an LPG cylinder for his college lecturer who had recently joined. That was Vikram - always eager and willing to help anyone in need.

While in college, Vikram was selected to undergo a forty-day paratrooping training with his NCC (air-wing) unit for which he had to go to Pinjore Airfield and Flying Club, about 35 kilometres away from Chandigarh. He asked me for a motorbike for his daily travelling to and from Pinjore. Since riding a motorbike was a craze among college students in those days, I managed the funds and bought him one, though in retrospect I realize he got to use it very little.

Unstoppable Vikram being awarded his graduation degree

It was only after attending the Republic Day parade as a NCC cadet in 1994, in New Delhi, that he told us about his wish to join the Indian Army. He was hugely impressed with the discipline and devotion to duty of the armed forces. The lifestyle of army officers had convinced him to take up a career in the army.

Earlier too, Vikram was selected for a job in Merchant Navy with a Hong Kong-based shipping company after a written test and a round of personal interviews in Bombay (Mumbai). He was on the verge of joining the precoast training in Madras (Chennai); even his tickets were booked. Three days before leaving for Madras, Vikram had second thoughts. He totally dropped the idea of joining Merchant Navy. He confided to his mother, 'Money is not everything in life; I have to do something bigger in life, something great, something extraordinary, which may bring fame to my country.'

***

Bonds that last forever: Mr popular Vikram with his college friends

Years later, the Indian Oil Corporation, one of the largest oil companies, paid tribute to Vikram in one of their advertisements: 'Sometimes an ordinary Indian can make a ₹1,20,000 crore company feel humble for every step we take...there's an inspired Indian leading the way.'

Vikram, as many would say later, was a gift to the motherland and its people. He had promised that he would lay down his life or win the battle for his country. Ironically and unfortunately, he kept both his promises.

***

One of his friends from college days, Avinash Kamath, even wrote an obituary after Vikram's martyrdom in an article tided A Gentlemen Forever' in *The Times of India.* He wrote 'What made this chap (Luv) from Palampur stand out in the crowd was his warmth, a proverbial friend in need whom you could always trust.

For Luv every friend was Veeru (brother).' He further wrote, 'Joining the forces was then a craze among us. Reasons: the glamour, a sense of adventure, discipline and the chance to be a gentleman forever. For Luv (Vikram) it was obsession. 'We live by chance, love by choice and kill by profession' was his favourite line. A Hindi movie about a gentleman cadet's life in the Indian Military Academy, Dehradun, settled the issue. 'If it's going to be the Army, it's going to be a permanent commission,' he announced after watching it. '

Such was the popularity Vikram gained after his martyrdom that *India Today* in one of its editions included his name in an all-India contest with four other luminaries of the country and asked its readers to put them in order of merit as people who have made India go 'wow' since 1975 from among Vikram, Indira Gandhi, Rajiv Gandhi, Atal Bihari Vajpayee (for Operation Shakti) and Rakesh Sharma (the astronaut).

THE CALLING

We live by chance, love by choice and kill by profession.

Vikram was very clear from his college days about his dream of joining the Army. An exasperated botany professor, while objecting to his irregular work once remarked, 'Your practical files are incomplete. You have not been attending the lectures and I have not seen you in the laboratory. What will you do in life?' Vikram by then had already found his calling in life. He answered calmly with full confidence, 'I will join the army, Sir!'

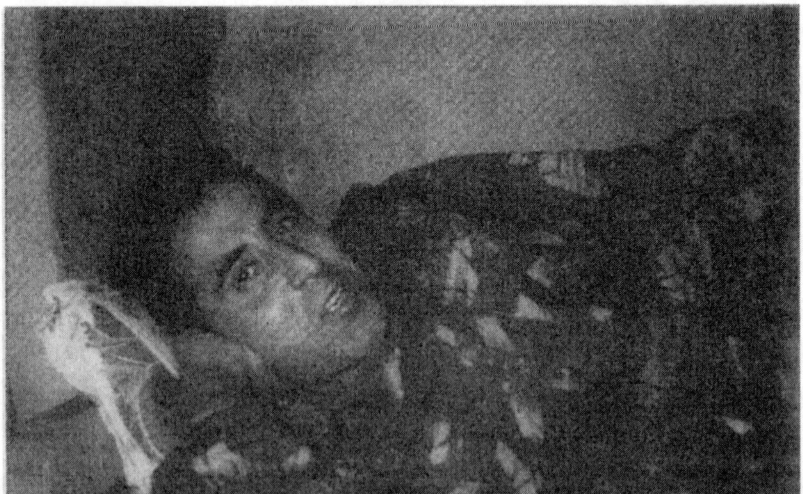

Dream comes true: Vikram had only one ambition - to join the army

In top form: Receiving an award for meritorious work

True to his words, he passed out of college and was adjudged the best NCC (air wing) cadet of Punjab Directorate in North Zone during the Inter-State NCC Camp.

He qualified for 'C' certificate and became a Senior Under Officer in his NCC unit and was handpicked to participate in the Republic Day parade in New Delhi in 1994.

After his college, Vikram decided to stay in Chandigarh and prepare for a career in the Army. He and his friend, Avinash Kamath, joined MA (English) course at Punjab University. Vikram opted for the evening classes and decided to take up a job in a private company in the morning. His friend recalls how Vikram did not want to burden me with the expense for his education. 'I don't want my father to foot my bills anymore,' he would say.

Regular and strenuous physical workouts, jogging and keeping abreast with the current events through newspapers became a part of his daily routine. He dedicated all his time to prepare for the

Seen here with a group of friends

A moment to celebrate: Vikram partying with his colleagues at the time of the Republic Day Parade, New Delhi

CDS (Combined Defense Services) examination. This left him with no time to study for his MA exams. As he had filled the examination form and paid the fee, at my insistence he wrote the exam. An underprepared Vikram was clear about what he wanted in life and so wrote 'Jai Bharat' on most of the answer sheets.

In 1996, Vickram qualified for the CDS exam as was expected. He fared well and was in the top 35 in the order of merit. He received a call from the Services Selection Board for an interview at Allahabad and got selected. Vikram was ecstatic and elated. He could see his dream being fulfilled. He was put under the infantry battalion.

No vision and you perish,
No ideal and you are lost,
Your heart must ever cherish,
Some faith at any cost,
Some hope, some dream to cling to,
Some rainbow in the sky,
Some melody to sing to,
Some service that is high!

– Harriet d'Autremont

Vikram had found his purpose in life. He had found the way to a righteous path that would lead him to his goal - to a service that was extraordinarily high and supreme.

PATH FORWARD

What you are is God's gift to you. what you become is your gift to God.

Vikram joined the Indian Military Academy (IMA), Dehradun, in June 1996 as a Gentleman Cadet in the Manekshaw Battalion. He was the most enthusiastic and a disciplined cadet in the Academy.

I am assuming as his school was located inside the Army Cantonment in Palampur, the olive green colour was permanently etched in his mind. It was a dream come true for him to have joined the Indian Army. He was all set for his 19-month training.

A proud moment: Wards of Gentlemen Cadets watching the Passing Out Parade

Always a loving and responsible sibling, Vikram performing a ritual during his sister's marriage

For him getting up at 4 a.m. was the most difficult part of the training. Everyone had to report for the 5-a.m. physical training. Vikram would say, 'The more you sweat in peace, the less you bleed in the war.' His favourite game of table tennis was now replaced by squash. He was very positive about the academy and the overall environment and was full of praises for the manner in which they were trained.

***

However, he was also sensitive towards his family responsibilities. While Vikram was at the academy, we had found a groom for our second daughter, Neetu, and finalized the marriage plans. The ceremony was to take place in New Delhi. Vikram was in a fix as cadets were not allowed to take leave even for a single day during the training period. He expressed his dilemma to his immediate commander. Owing to his brilliant track record, Vikram was given

Posted at Sopore: In the line of duty

At Dal Lake: Trying his hand at a motorboat

Braving it out during the floods in Baramulla: Doing his duty in times of natural calamities like floods

Vikram with a fellow officer's son: An inspiration for the younger generation

A force to reckon with: Vikram during his training days

Letting his guard down: Vikram takes a break with a colleague

Gearing up: Vikram during his IMA traing days

A gentlemen forever: Vikram, always a fauji at heart, was ecstatic on clearing his exam and joining the Indian Army

Wearing pride on his shoulders: Vikram shows Vishal around the IMA campus

special permission to attend the marriage. Vikram promised his commander to be back next morning before sunrise.

Vikram left for Delhi from Dehradun on the morning of 12 February only in time to attend the marriage. He managed to be present on the most important day of his sister's life. He left within a few hours and reported back to the Academy on 13th February morning before sunrise. He had kept his word.

Once Vishal, his brother fondly recalls, had also gone to meet him at the Academy. Vikram showed him around, explained to him their daily routine, and proudly introduced him to all his friends and fellow cadets.

Vikram was an enthusiastic and zealous cadet. He always had clarity of thought and took his trainings very seriously. But once the day was over, he would entertain his friends and laugh heartily. He had an infectious and uncontrollable laughter. Vikram would throw his head back, shake it involuntarily and his eyes would twinkle and his laughter would echo down the corridor. He lived every moment to its fullest and believed that life is a gift that's not to be wasted.

Through his vivacious nature, he created indelible memories and his teachers and seniors remember him vividly and fondly. In one of the letters, I had written to him during his training days. I had said that the ideals and principles he learns during his training at IMA would make him a fine army officer. Vikram always kept this letter in his pocket along with his eye donation card. He had pledged his eyes at the young age of 18.

Vikram passed out of the IMA on 6 December 1997. The entire family attended the passing out parade and the pipping ceremony. It was a very proud moment for all the cadets; they had now become young lieutenants and officers. Their eyes were lit with pride, a sense of achievement and higher purpose in life. Vikram proudly introduced us to his fellow cadets, officers and seniors.

We were overwhelmed with joy to be a part of the ceremony and to be associated with the family of an army officer. Vikram had etched the motto of IMA in his mind, body and soul. He lived by this motto and it reflected in his actions. Vikram had personalized this ideal and left his footprints in the sands of time, to be followed, preached and idolized.

And how true is this stanza from *Psalm of Life* by HW Longfellow of his life.

Lives of great men, all remind us
We can make our lives sublime
And, departing, leave behind us
Footprints on the sands of time.

FIRST POSTING

No one can have a good clean character if he does not have clean thoughts. If your aim is nobility you must have noble thoughts. If your desire is to be of service, you must think of ways you can serve others. If you want to be a radiant and beloved individual you must be a loving, kind, generous and appreciative person. If you want to know joy and peace of heart then you must think and try to maintain a joyous spirit.

After passing out from IMA Dehradun, Vikram was sent for a regimental training to Jabalpur, Madhya Pradesh, in December 1997. It was a 30-day training and he returned by the end of January 1998.

Thereafter, Vikram got his first posting at Sopore – the strife-torn town of Jammu & Kashmir's Baramulla district. He was commissioned as a Lieutenant in 13 Jammu & Kashmir Rifles. He was really excited about his posting at Sopore, a hotbed of terrorism in those days. News of infiltration was a daily affair and Indian soldiers sacrificing their lives protecting the borders was something what one would often hear. Though we were anxious about his posting in J&K, Vikram wasn't. He always used to say when you get commissioned in the forces, a bullet is made in your name but whether you get that bullet or not is your destiny and to die a soldier's death is an honour than to die otherwise. He joined his unit soon after.

In mid-March 1998, Vikram was sent for the course, a training of young officers, at the Infantry School, Mhow, Madhya Pradesh.

Boots, Belts, Berets: Vikram Batra holding the trophy on his company being declared the best

It was a five-month training; he returned in September 1998.

Vikram joined his unit in Sopore in October 1998. He would visit us often at Palampur during his Sopore posting. During those breaks he would share stories of encounters with terrorists. While one of those encounters when Vikram was in a dense forest leading an ambush with his fellow soldiers, a bullet whizzed past his right ear and hit the soldier behind him. It made him realize that the bullet was meant for him and not for his colleague. He ordered the platoon to nab each of the terrorist, and by morning all had been killed.

Such combats with terrorists gave him a reputation of a daredevil who did not fear death. He believed in leading from the front and was a caring commander.

***

Apart from being an able officer, Vikram enjoyed the company of his friends. His college friend Avinash remembers fondly a time, just before Kargil, when he tried to contact Vikram during his posting at Sopore. His call wasn't connected due to security reasons, but Vikram had called back on a Sunday afternoon. 'Sorry Veeru, couldn't contact you earlier. Things here are getting a little serious. But I am sure the situation will become normal soon. I have been promised a posting at a family station. I am planning to get married then. And one great news, I have presented a car to my dad,' he said, promising to call back soon.

***

In January 1999, Vikram was sent for a Commando Course at Belgaum (Karnataka) for two months. Vishal recalls how Vikram and his dear friend Sandhu came to VishaPs Lajpat Nagar one-room flat in New Delhi on 26 January 1999 and stayed over for a day. Vishal was working as an executive with Tata Finance in New Delhi at that time. Vikram used to relish butter chicken and asked him to take them to a good restaurant where he could have his favourite dish. At a small chicken corner underneath the Lajpat Nagar flyover, all three spent the entire evening eating and talking about army life and Sandhu gave Vikram tips for his commando course. The night just went by conversing. Vishal and Sandhu went to New Delhi railway station to see off Vikram.

Vikram excelled at the training. The determined and disciplined

Vikram, owing to his exceptional performance, was rewarded with the highest grading - the Instructor's Grade.

Determine and disciplined: Vikram excelled at all the courses at the academy

While on his way back from Belgaum, Vikram again dropped by at Delhi on 9 March 1999 to meet his brother Vishal. It was like a ritual; the brothers shared a strong bond and would catch up as often as they could. In the meantime that Vikram had gone for his commmando course, Vishal had tried his hand at driving. So, when Vishal took his cousin's car to pick him up, Vikram was quite surprised to see Vishal at the steering wheel.

Vishal recalls it to be a very emotional meeting. There was a lot to say and share. Vikram narrated all the stories of his two-month course and the fact that he enjoyed every bit of it (Vishal had also dreamt of joining the armed forces but, unfortunately, could not clear the SSB interview). The twins chatted through the night and before they realized, it was time for Vikram to say goodbye.

Time was a constraint as Vikram had to leave immediately for Palampur and then to Sopore. He also had to stop midway at Chandigarh to meet his girlfriend, Dimple.

Vishal went to see him off, in his cousin's car, to the bus terminus at New Delhi. It was a 40-minute drive. Vishal had no inkling that he was driving for the last time. Vishal still recollects that warm embrace, which is to stay with him for the rest of his life. Vikram waving goodbye with a huge smile will always remain etched in

Vishal's heart.

The commando training at Belgaum was an excruciating one. When Vikram came to Palampur post his training, I saw long red marks on his body. Vikram explained that during the training, they had to jump from a flying helicopter with a rope tied around his body, which kept rotating and, therefore, those marks. Vikram very casually played down my concern by saying that it was a part of training that every armyman has to go through. I always told him that no matter what, he must always be the best at whatever he chose to do. Vikram was living his dream.

Determination personified: Lucky are those who live their dream

Vikram came home, for the last time, for Holi of 1999. His mother made his favourite dishes - *rajma chawal, gobhi pakoda,* homemade potato chips and mango pickle, and packed some pickle for him and his colleagues too. It was a send-off like never before.

At the bus stand, when we, along with his friends, were seeing him off, we didn't know that it was the last time we were seeing our beloved Vikram; he was going away, never to return.

TUMULTUOUS TIMES

Awake! Arise and stop not tilt goal is achieved.

I recall the days vividly when Pakistan was repeatedly escalating tention on the Indo-Pak border. Time and again they deceived India by breaking an agreement wherein both sides had decided to withdraw from their bunkers during winter and re-occupy them only in spring. This was a decision that India and Pakistan had agreed upon mutually.

The then Pakistan prime minister, Nawaz Sharif, had expressed his desire for peace between the two countries to India's then prime minister, Atal Bihari Vajpayee, on the latter's visit to Pakistan in 1999. In accordance with the Lahore Declaration, the India Army had withdrawn their troops from the bunkers. Pakistani Army, however, stealthily continued to occupy the bunkers during the winter of 1999, with the mala fide intention of invading Kashmir. They pushed their troops towards the Kargil sector. This was their third attempt at infringing the Indian border.

In the first week of May 1999, Indian patrol parties discovered troops of Pakistani Army occupying our posts in Drass and the adjoining areas. The enemy was in a striking position to obstruct the Srinagar-Kargil-Leh National Highway, which is of utmost importance to India. Their immediate plot was to cut off the passage to Ladakh from Kashmir to isolate Kargil. The enemies' final target was to occupy Kashmir.

Fearless and unstoppable: Vikram and his colleagues patrol the borders at night

This was the third time that the Kargil invasion was planned by Pakistan. The first one was planned in 1987 but the enemy side could not carry it out due to their military and political shortcomings. It was again planned in 1997, when Nawaz Sharif was the prime minister and Pervez Musharraf, the General Officer Commanding of the Army Staff. It had failed then as well.

On 15 May 1999, the ambushing of an Indian patrol team led by Capt. Saurabh Kalia, who acted on a tip-off by a local shepherd in the Batalik sector, exposed the infiltration. The Pakistani forces ignoring the directives of Amnesty International and International and Human Rights Commission brutally tortured and killed the Indian patrol team.

The Pakistan Army returned the bodies of the patrol leader Capt. Saurabh Kalia, another boy from Palampur, and five soldiers, which enraged the entire country.

The Indian Army decided to retaliate. The enormity of the situation was understood when the Indian Army came to know that die Pakistani troops had actually entrenched themselves concretely at approximately 140 posts in the area, and it was almost impossible to dislodge the intruders sitting on such fortified heights. The Pakistani Army was well prepared for a battle and had the full support of its artillery with anti-aircraft guns, missiles, mortars and all sorts of heavy weapons.

India had to pay a heavy price for the slackness on part of vigilance, and yet the inadequacy of prior information of the enemy strength could not shatter the indomitable willpower of our bravehearts.

It was during this time, when the war broke out with Pakistan that Vikram's unit, 13 JAK Rifles, was instructed to ignore their previous command of moving to Shahjahanpur in Uttar Pradesh and to proceed to Kargil. On 1 June 1999, his unit proceeded to the

(L) In the eye of a storm: Vikram assesses the situation. (R) Posed for action: Vikram Vikram before a Pinaka Multi-barrel Rocket Launcher

Kargil sector. Vikram informed us about his movement. He reassured us and promised to call once in 10 days during the battle period.

Vikram knew that this was his testing time and that he must not fail his country. He believed in service above self, in novelty of thoughts and in the purity of heart, and coupled with determination to achieve the best, our hero stepped on the path from where there was no return.

Footprints, that perhaps another,
Sailing over life's solemn main,
A forlorn and shipwrecked brother,
Seeing, shall take heart again...

– HW Longfellow

TRIUMPH OVER THE HUMP ROCKY KNOB

We. in the Delta Company, were asked to capture Rocky Knob. Our chaps were highly motivated and our commanding officer had put so much spirit in us that there was no looking back. We were waiting to go up.

The Kargil War in 1999, which is believed to be one of the toughest wars ever fought in the world, was the field of action for Vikram; particularly Drass and Mashkoh valley were his action stations.

The Kargil sector is mainly divided into four sub-sectors: Drass, Mushkoh Valley, Batalik and Kaksar (Kargil). The Pakistani Army had crossed the Line of Control (LoC) and entered 10 to 15 kilometres into the Indian territory.

According to defence analysts, the intrusion started in the end of December 1998, as the Pakistanis had built bunkers with enough storage of arms and ammunition as well as food supplies. A few others believe that the intrusion might have started in May 1999, as soon as the snow melted, since these are steep and snow-bound peaks. On 14 May 1999, when the operation to flush out the enemy started, the number of intruders was about 300. Gradually, the

---

I tracked Vikram's achievements at Kargil through newspapers and magazines and through conversations with Vikram's friends and colleagues. Here I have made attempts to reconstruct the battle for the readers.

True strength: Senior army officers (U Lt Col YK Joshi and (M) Lt Gen. Amar Aul inspecting the situation, with [RJ Vikram looking on

number kept increasing and went up to around 1,500, with more and more joining them by June.

India was forced to launch Operation Vijay on 26 July 1999, because these were not just plain intruders but battalions of Pakistani Army, hired soldiers of different militant groups and fighting porters. It seemed a well-planned strategy to attack and defeat the Indian Army and stake claim over Kashmir.

The area of the Hump, Rocky Knob, Tololing and Point 5140 was of strategic importance to India. These were part of the Brass sub-sector. It included the highway leading from Srinagar to Leh from Zoji La onwards. It was a vital link and had to be kept open for the transportation of ammunitions and food material to further destinations.

Rajputana Rifles was tasked to clear the Tololing Peak with the support of artillery firing, a brigade in action with 120 guns firing directly. This peak was captured on 13 June at around 8 O'clock in the morning. Twelve soldiers, including officers, were killed in the final assault. It was the initial success of the armed forces, which paved the way for further victories. Taking control of the Tololing Peak changed the course of the war for India. The morale of the Indian army was boosted as they received applause and appreciation from all corners.

The operation was fully underway. The forces proceeded further beyond Tololing Peak for the recapture of the Hump feature heavily dominated by the enemy.

It is said that Brass is the second coldest inhabited place in the world after Siberia. The temperature falls down to -60°C in winter and the average altitude is 10,600 feet above sea level. It varies at

A tought terrain: Drass as seen from Hump VII

Honour above all: Officers of Teevra Terah, Totaling, after the victory

Battlefield at the top: Peak 5140 and the Hump feature

Against all odds: Vikram and his colleagues at the Hump feature

A strong soul: Perseverance and courage defined Vikram

A view of the Hump, Rocky Knob, Tololing and Point 5140 from the south-west frontier

different places from 12,000 to 18,000 feet across the Himalayan ranges.

There was a perennial cold breeze that pierced the lungs and extra effort was needed to even breathe and walk normally. The enemy was by this time well-ensconced in dominating positions, atop the mountains from where they could target the Indian soldiers. The armed forces had to face the enemy by climbing the peaks in such frosty and inhuman conditions to dislodge them.

Though Vikram's battalion had moved to Brass from Sopore in the first week of June, it was only on 12 June 1999 that they received their first order. Their first task was to act as a reserve for the forces fighting at the Hump. The Hump is an extension of the Tololing feature. The battalion fighting at the Hump had lost one of their young officers, Maj. Ajay Jastoria.

The soldiers of 13 JAK Rifles fought for two nights continuously and recaptured the positions over the Hump and Rocky Knob on

17 June 1999. In the'process, eight enemy soldiers were killed, nine wounded and a few fled leaving their guns and artillery behind.

Vikram had written to his brother Vishal, just before moving from Brass. He was sitting at a height of 15,500 feet and fighting the war with Pakistan. In his letter, Vikram had lovingly added, Take care of Mom and Bad.' He was full of enthusiasm and pride.

OPERATION VIJAY

I believe because it is impossible.

Point 5140 is at an altitude of over 17,000 feet. It is the highest peak on the ridge. This peak is of vital importance to the Indian side due to its proximity to Srinagar. One of the enemy helicopters was parked there to monitor the progress of the Indian Army, and unless it was captured no other helicopter could land there. Moreover, this point had direct access to the Srinagar-Leh

Ready for the war: Holding ground on the rugged terrain

A national hero: Vikram with an anti-aircraft gun briefing the media after the success at point 5140

Highway, and its capture could lead to further success for our Army.

The task of capturing this peak was assigned to B&D companies of 13 JAK Rifles. D Delta Company was commanded by Vikram and B Bravo, by Capt. SS Jamwal. Multi-barrel rocket launchers were replaced on Srinagar-Leh Highway facing towards Point 5140 to provide artillery support to Battalion Commander Lt Col YK Joshi. It was on the night of 19 June that both Vikram and Capt. Jamwal had been assigned to lead their respective companies for Point 5140.

They had to finish the task by the first ray of dawn. Both shook hands with Lt Col Joshi and proceeded towards their mission. They had only seven to eight hours to finish this task before dawn, when the Pakistani invaders could easily spot the movement of our troops climbing up. The enemy sitting at 17,000 feet were at an advantageous position whereas our soldiers had to climb the entire mountain peak to counter them. In an audacious move, Vikram decided to attack from the rear to surprise the Pakistanis. He ordered his men to climb the mountain as stealthily as possible and instructed them that even the sound of breathing should not be heard. The brave soldiers climbed the slippery slope in the dead of night, with the rocks covered with frozen rain and biting cold.

Carefully and cautiously, both the companies reached within a range of about 200-300 metres of Point 5140 unnoticed by the enemy. As the party was advancing, artillery firing was stopped, but the enemy sensed the troops' advancement and opened fire. Soon Vikram and Capt. Jamwal understood the situation and continued retaliating till they reached close to the point.

The calm was disrupted all of a sudden with the enemy opening fire on the Indian troops from the other end. The silence of the night was broken by the noise of bullets, guns and anti-aircraft guns. Amidst the attack from the enemy, the Bravo and Delta companies continued their upward movement towards Point 5140.

Due to his tough demeanour, Vikram was codenamed 'Sher Shah' by his colleagues, named after Sher Shah Suri. When Vikram was near his target, the enemy commander was heard on radio and warned him: 'Why have you come up Sher Shah? Not one of you will return back alive.' Vikram had never learnt to be afraid of any challenge. He immediately responded: 'Within one hour we will see who will remain on the top.'

True to their words that night, there was no stopping the Indian soldiers. They were full of anger and there was a great deal of determination in their actions. Their attack was so ferocious that it forced the Pakistanis to retreat. The soldiers kept shouting and motivating themselves with the war cries: 'We have to do it', 'We will take our revenge' and 'We will win'; and finally they did it.

During the attack, one of Capt. Jamwal's soldiers lost his hand. Jamwal pulled him behind a rock and bandaged his injured hand; both broke down as they held each other. Later I had read somewhere that this brave soldier was an excellent basketball player

Those who command themselves, command others: Vikram and his fellow soldiers taking a break after the capature of Point 5140

The men who won glory: (R) Capt. Jamal, (C) Lt Col Joshi and ID Vikram at Point 5140

and now he'd never be able to play his game again. Yet, this did not deter the spirit of our soldiers. Capt. Jamwal went back and joined Vikram in the attack.

Two bunkers on the top were captured first by Bravo Company led by Capt. Jamwal. At the same time, Vikram charged with his company and fired three rockets on the eastern bunkers. Vikram took the lead and attacked the nearest bunker with a hand grenade. He immediately moved to the next without stopping to see the situation at the top. Vikram was highly motivated, and inspired by his enthusiasm his troops attacked with renewed vigour. With their grit and valour, Vikram and Capt. Jamwal cleared all the seven bunkers showing exemplary courage. In the fierce fighting, eight Pakistani soldiers were killed, some got injured while others fled in the dark of night and fell from the rocky ridges to their death. Our troops captured a large quantity of arms, ammunition and even an anti-aircraft gun from the captured bunkers.

At 3.15 a.m., both the companies were at the peak after capturing two bunkers at the top and five in the east. It was 3.25 a.m. when Vikram looked at his watch; they were still left with an hour before the first light of dawn was to touch the peak at 4.30 a.m. Both the heroes had cleared all the seven bunkers with no sign of enemy soldier at the ridge. They had captured Point 5140, which heightened India's chances of winning the war.

When Capt. Jamwal radioed his victory signal, *Oh yeah, yeah, yeah* and Vikram with his, *Yeh dil maange more,* the Army Headquarters were ecstatic and filled with a sense of pride and joy.

CAPTURING POINT 5140

We are particularly grateful to Capt Batra for having used our Pepsi's well-known slogan Yeh Oil Maange More. He has immortalized this slogan and we ewe a lot to him.

Col Joshi was ecstatic on receiving the victory message from Vikram and Capt. Jamwal. He started moving towards the 9 peak because before going for the assault, both the young officers had promised to have their morning cup of tea at Point 5140 together. A wave of joy had spread across the Brigade and Army Headquarters in New Delhi. It was a historical achievement for the Indian Army as well as for India.

The Chief of Army, Gen. VP Malik, personally telephoned Vikram for their battalion's remarkable and almost impossible feat.

This was a decisive victory for 13 JAK Rifles at a height of 17,000 feet without a single soldier being killed in the battle. Col Joshi's eyes were moist as he said, 'Not a single soldier died in the operation. The victory of peak 5140 would make a textbook on mountain warfare for the manner in which the operation was carried out. A peak at 17,000 feet was literally snatched from the jaws of powerful enemy without a single soldier losing his life. This is God's grace and perfect execution of an operation by the youngsters who are the heart, mind and soul of the army.'

According to various reports, it was one of India's toughest campaigns in mountain warfare. To reach Point 5140, eight humps

A force to reckon with: The capture of point 5140 ensured India's victory in the Kargil War

had to be crossed. The Pakistanis had deployed machine guns on these peaks and also received artillery support from PoK (Pak occupied Kashmir). But, our valiant fighters achieved the impossible without sustaining any casualty. Vikram's men swore by his name. Photographs of Vikram and his battalion mounting on the captured Pakistani gun at the base camp were splashed across all the newspapers of the country.

Due to his exemplary and unbelievable feat, Vikram was awarded with many tides. He came to be fondly called as 'Tiger of Brass', 'Lion of KargiT, 'Kargil Hero' and so on. His bravery, zeal and determination had set a standard for everyone in the troop fighting the battle. He became a national hero.

After the victory at Point 5140, an enthusiastic and thrilled Vikram called us on the morning of 20 June 1999.1 received his call and he very excitedly said, 'Daddy, I have captured my peak.' This was his first call after joining the warfield.

16-06-99

Dear Sushu,

Love & Hi there!

Its been very-very long since we've been in contact. Tried your office phone no umpteen times but to no avail. So how's life? Are you still working with SAPA or have you shifted to some new. And what happened of your 'BANK OF PANJAB' interview.

Regarding my side, after coming back from commando's stayed at my old loc for around three months. As you've been reading and listening the news daily, things have gone very hot here. I am sitting at a height of 15,000 feet and fighting the war with Paki's. I can't write you the name of the place because of security measures.

Life is at total risk. Anything can happen here, everyday facing hell lot of bullets and only shells. Today is very sad day for our battalion as we have lost one officer. I can't write you the name of the officer. He was my senior subaltern (i.e immediate senior). So everyone is very sad today. Rest everything is fine this end.

Dear Sushu, take care of mom & dad, as I have already written you that anything can happen here. So convey my love to dear Mom & Dadi and Jijaji. How is mona. Say my hi to her. And do talk to dimple once and say my love to her. Don't know when I'll come back, as leave of all pers of NC have been cancelled.

Nothing more to write so I pen down. Miss you all a lot. Take care & God bless. So write me back, as I'll get the letter & do tell dimple also to pen down to me. Hope I shall see you all soon. Till then Good-bye.

Lots of Love

Brother

Luv

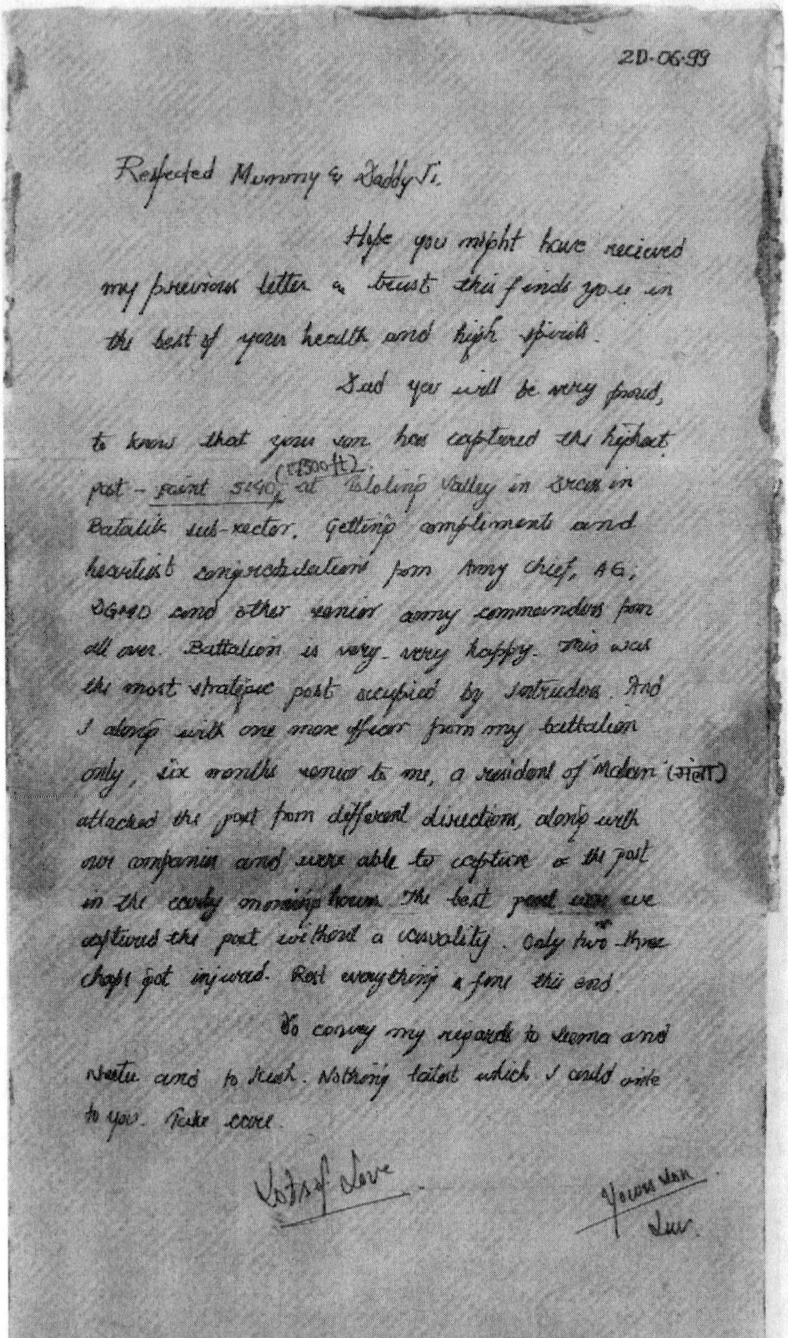

20-06-99

Respected Mummy & Daddy Ji,

Hope you might have recieved my previous letter & trust this finds you in the best of your health and high spirits.

Dad you will be very proud, to know that your son has captured the highest post – point 5140 (17500 ft) at Tololing Valley in Dras in Batalik sub-sector. Getting compliments and heartiest congratulations from Army chief, AG, DGMO and other senior army commanders from all over. Battalion is very-very happy. This was the most strategic post occupied by intruders. And I along with one more officer from my battalion only, six months senior to me, a resident of Malan (मंला) attacked the post from different directions, along with our companies and were able to capture the post in the early morning hours. The best part was we captured the post without a casuality. Only two-three chaps got injured. Rest everything is fine this end.

Do convey my regards to Seema and Neetu and to Kush. Nothing latest which I could write to you. Take care.

Lots of love.

Your son
Luv.

23.06.99

Dearest Kush,

Hi! Trust this letter finds you in the best of your health and high spirits. Hope you've received my previous letter which I wrote at Mori's add. I am writing you this letter from point 5140 (at Tololing) which you might be hearing about everyday in the news. Yeah, you will be proud to know that we've captured it. Lt Jamwal (you met at Shimla) and I had gone to attack it and we captured ~~it~~ it on 20th killing 8 pakis and captured hell lot of arms & ammn. Whole battalion is very happy on our performance. We both have been recommended for MVC (Mahavir Chakra) for this task. And I have also picked up the rank of captain.

Yesterday I had called up Mummy & Daddy from this place as we had got satellite telephone for some time, so everyone got a chance to speak at their place. I've also received letters from Nippy, Nippy's parents, Omkar. Rest everything is fine this end. Dont know about leave plan. Do give a call to Dimple and tell her about me that I am fine and tell about my achievement also. We have got congratulatory calls from Army Chief, AG, DGMO and other army cdrs from all over. Nothing more to write so I pen down. Do reply soon. I am sitting at a height of 17200 ft. Sorry for hand, as it's very cold here.

Love Always

Yours
Luv!

The satellite phone line was not clear and his words muffled. He re-assured me that he was fine and that he had achieved success in his task. His mother blessed him and encouraged him to continue performing his duty and never look back. And look back he did not.

A NATION REJOICES ITS HERO

All the great things are simple, and many can be expressed in a single word: freedom, justice, honor, duty, mercy, hope. - Winston Churchill

Post the victory over Point 5140, Vikram became a national hero. Stories of his heroic deeds were being telecasted on TV in the entire country. For four days, Vikram was on TV, recalling his saga of bravery, telling journalists how he led his men to victory, capturing enemy bunkers on Point 5140. The newspapers carried pictures of weapons seized from the intruders by Vikram and his men. Not just his Battalion and the Indian Army, but the entire nation was inspired and felt proud of his victory. The manner in which he decided to take on the enemy position behind a rock, barging towards the machine gun nested on top, under its murderous fire had left the entire nation speechless.

Keeping true to his indominable spirit, Vikram along with five of his men climbed on. First, he crawled towards the enemy machine gun nest and hurled two grenades. As three enemy soldiers rushed out of their hideout, he singlehandedly engaged them in close fire fight, killing them all. He regrouped his men on the top and led them onto attacking defences. Leading from the front, he rallied his men and pressed on the attack till they captured Point 5140 by early morning.

Great leaders inspire: With that affable smile, so distinctive of Vikram, he ratlied his men and pressed on the attack

This act of bravery had inspired every citizen of the country, particularly the younger generation who made Vikram Batra a youth icon. Stories of his bravery and valour now became a household discussion. He had managed to infuse an immense sense of patriotism into the hearts of every Indian who heard his story.

Barkha Dutt, a senior journalist covering the Kargil War, interviewed Vikram after the victory over Point 5140. She had asked Vikram how he felt after his victory to which he famously said *Yeh dil maange more* with a big smile. He was brimming with confidence; a pleasant smile on his face and high energy levels indicated a sense of pride, I guess.

After the victory, Vikram had become a toast of the media as he appeared in a number of interviews; his bravery became the nation's story. In one of those interviews, he had told the news reporters that while capturing Point 5140, they were just 50 meters away from the target when right in front of them was a patch of snow. When the enemy started firing illumination rounds. Vikram and his troops had to lay down there pretending to be dead as the enemy were using machine guns and rockets.

With the capture of Point 5140, the course of battle was turned towards further victories and the morale of our army was boosted. His name was also recommended for Maha Vir Chakra award, the second-highest gallantry award of the country.

In the meantime, the enemy continued its firing. The troops retaliated with automatic guns but were pinned down by heavy firing from the other side. It was crucial to capture Point 4875. The point had to be reinforced, and now Lt Col Joshi had to decide who would head the mission.

Fresh from the victory, Vikram again volunteered to lead the troops. It is believed that using the tired troops in operations again and again is dangerous, but when the operations are continuous, there is no alternative left.

Such was the zeal and enthusiasm of the soldiers that despite strict rules, where soldiers cannot question the orders of their seniors, several soldiers literally pleaded for permission to accompany Vikram even at the cost of earning severe displeasure of the commanding officer.

Brimming with confidence and high energy levels: Vikram possessed an immense sense of pride

Soldiers were so enthused with Vikram's volunteering act that they were willing to be court martialled for the sake of accompanying Vikram.

Vikram by now had earned the respect of every soldier in the Army and his determination and bravery went on to be a saga in front of the whole nation.

BATTLE OF POINT 4875

Don't walk behind me, I may not lead you.
Don't walk in front of me. I may not follow you.
Walk beside me and be my friend.

After the capture of Point 5140, the troops (led by Vikram and Capt. Jamwal) had to station there for a few days, as there were chances of counter-attack by the enemy. They stayed at the top till June 26 to strengthen the defence and reshape the bunkers. They returned to the base camp to rest and re-energize for a few days. They could not rest for more than three to four days as the condition on other peaks were worsening and Point 4875 had

NH 1A between Mina Marg and Matayen as seen from Point 4875

02 JULY '89.

Respected Daddy & Mummy Ji,

Trust this letter finds you in the best of your health. Hope you might have recieved my earlier two letters.

Regarding my side I am fine here by the grace of almighty. I'd come down to Dras from top for 5-6 days for rest and recoup, but again moving up today for another offensive action. So all set to go.

Had undertaken a very big operation earlier also, in which I got 100% success and it was the biggest success in this sector. So had also recieved congratulatory calls from Army Chief and other senior commanders from all over. Was also interviewed by the entire press media.

Dont know when I'll be moving down again, so whenever I'll get a chance, I will call you up. So do pray for the success of my next op. Nothing more news, so I pen down. Take care.

Love Always

Do Reply

Your Son

Luv!

Mission impossible: The final target. Point 4875

become a challenging task. To win Point 4875 was now absolutely essential for India.

Point 4875 was a next-to-impossible mission. The conditions prevailing at these heights were extreme to say the least and unimaginable. This peak was heavily impounded by the enemy, and the Pakistani artillery had its guns targeted at the whole stretch, of about 30-40 kilometres, of National Highway 1A from Drass to Matayen. Any vehicle passing through this route could be easily targeted and destroyed. Even helicopter landing had become impossible.

However, the Indian troops continued to hold their post. But it was soon evident that a fresh reinforcement of troops had to reach them. And this is when Vikram and his army of men were called in to assist the weray combatting troops. Even the Pakistanis had intercepted the wireless message where the base told the troops at the peak that Sher Shah would reach them soon.

Before going up for his final battle, Vikram wrote a letter to us. The tone of the letter was, without doubt, ecstatic. He wrote:

I am fine here by the grace of Almighty. I had come down to Dross from top for 5-6 days' rest and recuperated but P m again moving up today for another offensive action.. .so all set to go.

I had undertaken a very big operation earlier in which I got 100% success and it was a remarkable achievement in this sector. I had also received congratulatory calls from Army Chief and other senior commanders from all over and was also interviewed by the media.

Don't know when I will be moving down again, so whenever I will get a chance, I will call you up. So do pray for the successes of my next operation.

Both, my wife and I, read the letter and eagerly waited for our 24-year-old young and brave son to return and call home. And thus began our never-ending wait.

THE FINAL BATTLE

I will either come back after raising the Indian flag in victory or return wrapped in it.

The impending assignment, recapturing of Point 4875, was a near impossibility. It is even difficult to imagine the extreme conditions prevailing on those heights. This was one of the most difficult peaks - and the most crucial. Regaining it would strengthen India's hold on the Valley. The Pakistani artillery, stationed at the height of 17,000 feet, had trained its guns on the whole stretch of National Highway 1A from Brass to Matayen. Many of the brave truck drivers, who dared to move on this stretch, had become the target of the Pakistani artillery. However, even in these hostile conditions, the pilots managed to fly their helicopters at a very low height along the Pandrass Ridge.

***

Over the next few days, after coming back home from college, I would watch the evening news on TV to get any update on my son. I recall a TV correspondent who had managed to reach the base camp and interview Vikram had asked him to share his feelings. Vikram had replied, 'Our government is taking care of the supply of our food material and other things to the best of their abilities at such high altitude. It is a tough task. I also wish that the

After seizing Point 4875: Despite desultory conditions, a chopper lands on the peak

families of the deceased soldiers are looked after well by the government and society.' His commanders appreciated his mature reply (he was all of 24 years then and the youngest captain in the Kargil battlefield), but hundreds of miles away, at home, when I saw Vikram's facial expression on TV, my heart sank, as I could read the expression on his face. After speaking to the reporter, he just turned his face away from the camera. I turned away from the television screen and broke down as I doubted his safe return back home. I remember my wife asking me why I had gone so silent suddenly; I could not tell her what I felt.

***

On 1 July 1999, Lt Coljoshi and the commander of 'A' Company, Maj. S Vijay Bhaskar climbed to a high vantage point to take a full view of the area of operation and draw up an attack plan. Based on the report, the commander prepared a battle plan at the headquarters, 79 Mountain Brigades. On 2 July 1999, the battalion was taken to 1,500 meters below Point 4875 to an area, which offered some cover. The brave porters carried ammunitions and heavy weapons for the battalion to this area.

On 4 July, the battalion was showed their objectives by Company Commander Major Gurpreet Singh. At 6 p.m. the Bofors guns commenced their bombardment. At 8.30 p.m., in the night, the troops started the tortuous climb to the top at height of 17,000 feet. The thick fog made the movement more precarious at an 80 degree gradient. At such an altitude the air is so thin that one would find it difficult to breathe; the soldiers were panting. The troops were 200 meters short of their objective, when the enemy started heavy firing. The Indian troops began to retaliate with automatic guns, but they were pinned down by the heavy enemy fire. They were also in the imminent danger of being exposed as the daylight was approaching.

The enemy continued with heavy firing, which was reported to the Company Commander. On 5 July, Lt Coljoshi personally fired two Faggot missiles from the fire base. They were direct hits and the enemy could be seen fleeing. At 1 pm on 5 July 1999, our troops captured Point 4875.

But, the enemy continued to fire from a position north of Point 4875. It became evident that this post had to be conquered. A strong contingent of enemy troops could be seen on a long and narrow ledge running north of Point 4875. To secure our position, it was necessary to clear the ledge. The battle continued the entire day. On 6 July 1999, it was reported that our troops could not sustain firefighting of such intensity without reinforcements. The reinforcements were immediately brought up. A fresh wave of enthusiasm coursed through the exhausted troops at the top. Listening to the news of Vikram coming, the troops cheered. Vikram had already become a hero, and stories of his valour had spread across the army. Through the interception of the radio

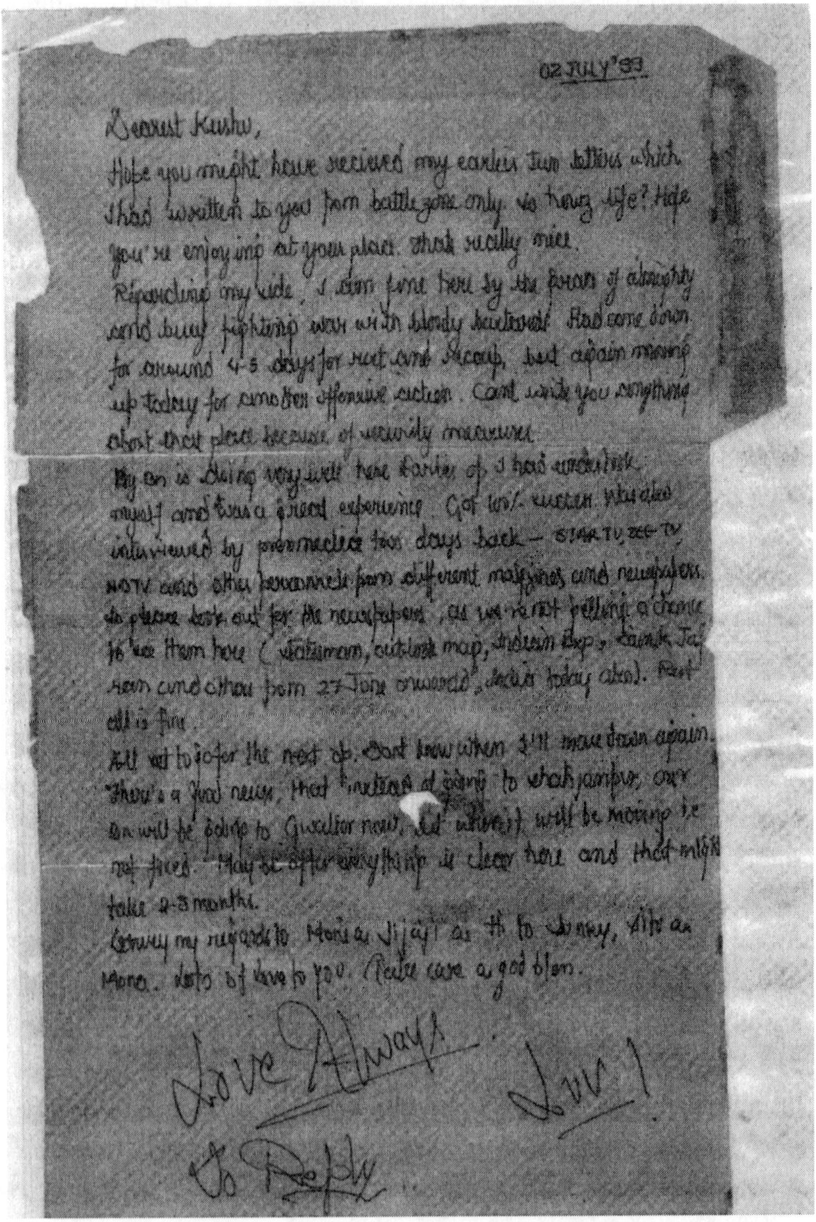

02 JULY '99

Dearest Kushu,

Hope you might have recieved my earlier two letters which I had written to you from battle zone only. Hows life? Hope you're enjoying at your place. That's really nice.

Regarding my side, I am fine here by the grace of almighty and busy fighting war with bloody [illegible]. Had come down for around 4-5 days for rest and recoup, but again moving up today for another offensive action. Cant write you anything about that place because of security measures.

My Bn is doing very well here. Earlier op I had undertook myself and was a great experience. Got 100% success. We also interviewed by press media two days back — STAR TV, ZEE TV, NDTV and other personnels from different magzines and newspapers. So please look out for the newspapers, as we're not getting a chance to see them here (Statesman, Outlook mag, Indian Exp, Dainik Jagran and others from 27 June onwards, and in today also). Rest all is fine.

All set to go for the next op. Dont know when I'll move down again. There's a [illegible] news, that instead of going to Shahjahanpur, our Bn will be going to Gwalior now, but when it will be moving i.e. not fixed. May be after everything is clear here and that might take 2-3 months.

Convey my regards to Mom & Vijay[illegible] & Hi to [illegible], [illegible] & Mona. Lots of love to you. Take care & god bless.

Love Always!

[illegible]

To Reply

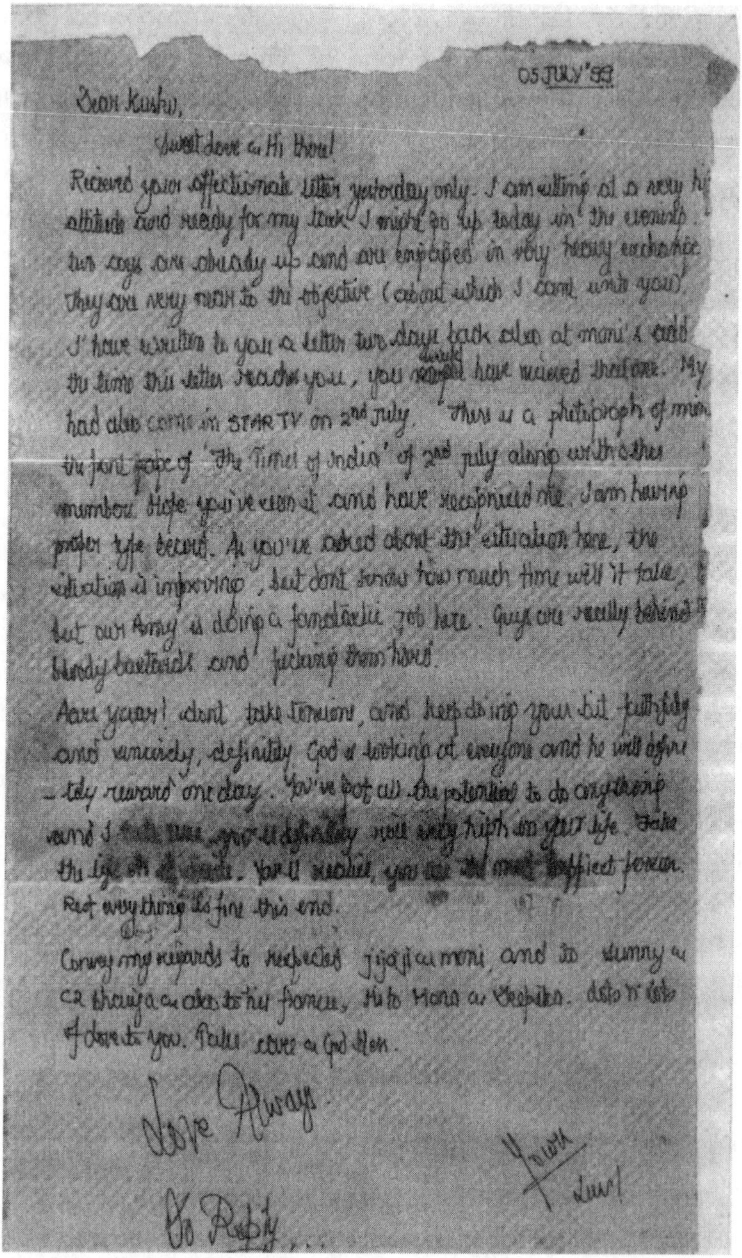

05 JULY '99

Dear Kushu,

Sweet love & Hi there!

Recieved your affectionate letter yesterday only. I am sitting at a very high altitude and ready for my task. I might go up today in the evening. Our coys are already up and are engaged in very heavy exchange. They are very near to the objective (about which I cant write you). I have written to you a letter two days back also at mom's add. By the time this letter reaches you, you would have recieved that one. My [illegible] had also come in STAR TV on 2nd July. There is a photograph of mine in the front page of 'The Times of India' of 2nd July along with other member. Hope you've seen it and have recognised me. I am having proper type beard. As you've asked about the situation here, the situation is improving, but dont know how much time will it take, but our Army is doing a fantastic job here. Guys are really bashing [illegible] bloody bastards and fucking them hard.

Aare yaar! dont take tension, and keep doing your bit faithfully and sincerely, definitely God is looking at everyone and he will defini-tely reward one day. You've got all the potential to do anything and I [illegible] sure, you'll definitely rise very high in your life. Take the life [illegible]. You'll realise, you are the most [illegible] person. Rest everything is fine this end.

Convey my regards to respected jijaji & mom, and to dunny & CR bhaiya & also to his fiancee, Hi to Mona & Deepika. Lots n' lots of love to you. Take care & God bless.

Love Always

to Ruby...

Yours

Luv!

frequencies, the enemy got a wind of Vikram's presence. Once again the enemy threatened him on his radio, 'Sher Shah upar toh aa gaye ho, lekin wapis nahi jane denge; Inshallah, upar hi bhej denge' (Sher Shah, you have come this far, but you will not go back alive. Inshallah, we'll kill you.) An undaunted Vikram replied, 'Upar toh tumhe aur tumhare sathiyon ko jana hoga' (You take care of yourself; you and your companions will be killed.)

Sitting amidst bursting shells and grenades, Vikram wrote his last letter to his twin brother:

'Dear Kushu,
I am sitting at a very high altitude and ready for my task. I might go up today in the evening. Two coys (companies) are already up and are engaged in very heavy exchange. They are very near to the objective about which I can't write to you... The situation is improving, but don't know how much time it will take, but our army is doing a fantastic job here.'

On 6-7 July, Vikram volunteered to head a party and reach this ledge even though he was unwell. Due to high fever and fatigue, his eyes were red as he sat wrapped in a blanket. His commanding officer hesitated to send him to the battlefront seeing Vikram's condition, but Vikram insisted. Hearing their hero's offer, many soldiers volunteered to accompany him. Vikram and the soldiers began their arduous trek. From eyewitnesses I had heard later that while still at the task, somewhere along the climb suddenly Vikram's face changed. The sign of fatigue and fever vanished. He became a man fired by a mission.

The chilling winds of Mushkoh Valley penetrated the bones of our soldiers. It was pitch dark. The climb was almost vertical. To make matters worse it began snowing. Vikram continued to move like a snow leopard. He coaxed and encouraged his exhausted troops to press on. Then he heard the rat-a-tat of a machine gun, which had pinned down his troops. Vikram swiftly moved towards the firing gun by hiding behind a rock and then ran to the shelter of the next till he reached close to the gun and lobbed a hand grenade and destroyed it. He then asked his troops to follow him. They advanced to the next position since the enemy guns had to be silenced before daylight.

Yet the Indian troops went forward without stopping, as if some supernatural power was propelling them. Two more enemy guns had to be silenced before dawn. It seemed an impossible task.

When Vikram had volunteered for this assignment he must have known that it might cost him his life but such was his enthusiasm that no such thought bothered him. He moved ahead, firing constantly with his AK-47. Fearlessly he closed in on the enemy. It was a fight at such close quarters that he could not even use his rifle. He pulled out his bayonet and charged at the enemy. Vikram grappled with a Pakistani soldier. He floored him with a punch on the nose and plunged his bayonet in him. Another intruder attacked him from behind. Vikram threw him off his back and pierced him with his bayonet. A machine gun was firing from the ledge. Vikram plunged inside the ledge where two soldiers were feeding the gun and a soldier was firing it. A junior officer of the Pakistani Army was supervising them. Vikram leaped inside and single-handedly killed all five of them. However, he was outnumbered and was shot at close range.

Unnerved by the fury of the attack, the Pakistanis fell back. The Indian soldiers gained an upper hand. Captain Batra's sacrifice paved the way for success of our troops and consolidate the Indian hold on Point 4875.

THE MARTYRDOM

The safety, honour and welfare of your country come first always and every time.
The honour, welfare and comfort of the men you command come next
Your own ease, comfort and safety come last, always and every time.

Vikram, with another young officer, Anuj Nayyar, fought off the enemy's counter-attack ferociously. They cleared all the enemy bunkers, egged their men forward, engaged in hand-to-hand combat and forced the Pakistanis to retreat. On 7 July, the mission was almost over when Vikram ran out of his bunker to rescue another officer, Lt Naveen Anaberu, whose legs were severely injured in an explosion. The Subedar of his battalion begged him not to go and offered to go instead. But Vikram famously told him, 'Tu baal-bachchedar hai, hat ja peeche.' (You have a wife and children. Step aside.) He lunged forward to save the young Lt Naveen Anaberu. As Vikram was dragging Naveen towards cover, the gravely wounded officer pleaded with Vikram to let him continue the fight. Just then a bullet pierced through Vikram's chest. Vikram was martyred but he managed to save the life of Lt Naveen.

***

Gaurav Sawant in his book Dateline Kargil writes, 'Vikram Batra had succeeded in clearing the ledge, securing the peak and also securing the movement of the 17 Jat troops pinned down by effective

Man of honour and extraordinary courage: Vikram Batra s name will inspire generations to come

Pakistani firing. Under the guidance of Colonel Dinesh Badola, jawans of the Second Battalion of the Naga Regiment advanced silently at night to capture the Twin Bumps. Mounting a ruthless attack, the Nagas dislodged the Pakistani soldiers. Once Nagas took Twin Bumps, Pakistani forward troops .did not get reinforcements, weapons and ammunition. They were choked and left with no option but to retreat.'

Another TV journalist, Srinjoy Chowdhury, covering the war writes in his book *Despatches from Kargil,* 'Vikram would volunteer for the most difficult tasks, climbing up a sheer rockface to take the enemy in the rear. And how thin the margins between death and glory are! This time there was no return to adulation, no TV cameras, just a few tears and a letter home. A hidden machine-gun opened up; he crawled up and silenced it with a volley of grenades. When three enemy soldiers rushed out, he killed them all, but was seriously wounded in the firefight. He refused to be evacuated; he would regroup his men and charge towards the final defences, dying in the effort. They didn't give him the Param Vir Chakra for nothing.'

Those who survived, later reported that Vikram died with the words, 'Jai Mata Di' (Victory to Mother Durga!) on his lips.

***

We received the news of Vikram's martyrdom on 8 July. My wife, Kamal Kanta, had just returned from her school when our neighbours informed her that two military officers had come but there was no one at home. She cried out in fear because she knew that military officers generally come to announce some bad news. She prayed with all her heart before she dialled my number. She told me about the army officers' visit and asked me to come home immediately. When I reached home and saw the officers I sensed that Vikram was no more. I asked the two officers to wait before they tell me anything. I went straight to my *puja* room, and prayed for a while. When I came out of the room, one of the officers stepped out, took my hand and said, 'Batra Saheb, Vikram is no more.' I collapsed hearing the news.

***

The day his body was brought home it was excruciating. With tears coursing down her cheeks, my wife said, 'No parent can see the dead body of their young son. Our son had captured three peaks, he had taken the nation by storm but suddenly he was no more. Yet, when God gives you a mortal blow, he gives you the strength to cope with the grief. Guru Govind Singh sacrificed four sons for the country. May be there was some reason that God gave me twins - one had been marked for the country and one for me.'

***

VICTORY HAS ITS PRICE

The main issue in life is not victory but the fight.
The essential thing is not have won but to have fought well.

Enraged by his death, the soldiers of 13 JAK Rifles pursued the enemy. A soldier from the battalion told Gaurav Sawant, a TV correspondent covering the war, 'Nobody was bothered about the bullets flying in any direction. There was only one thing in everybody's mind: to avenge Capt. Batra's death. We followed the fleeing soldiers. Such was their fear that some of them fell to

Have the courage of one's conviction: Officers and jawans of Teevra Terah with the captured guns at Point 4875

THE TIMES OF INDIA

New Delhi, Friday, July 2, 1999 • Late City

News flash: The heroic tale of Vikram and his soldiers got extensive media coverage

their death while fleeing.'

After routing the enemy, the Indian soldiers came back and sat surrounding the body of their beloved 'Sher Shah'. It was hard for them to believe that the dynamo, who was energizing, inspiring and coaxing them a little while back, was no more.

By the morning of 8 July 1999, India had won Point 4875 but lost Capt. Vikram Batra.

With the conquest of Point 4875, the connectivity to Ladakh was secured and our vehicles could now move freely on the Srinagar-Leh Highway.

Capt. Anuj Nayyar of 17 Jat Regiment had left his watch and a diamond ring with Vikram before setting off for the operation. He never returned to reclaim them. He too was martyred while clearing the fourth bunker.

India won the battle but lost about 524 of its brave soldiers; with 1,363 being seriously injured. The battle was won entirely because of the patriotic fervour and zeal of the young officers. Great achievements never come without great sacrifices.

Today, Point 4875 has been renamed as 'Captain Batra Top', and the transit camp in Brass where weary soldiers break their journey has come to be known as Capt. Batra Transit Camp. Capt. Anuj Nayyar was awarded the Maha Vir Chakra, the second highest award for bravery. For his sustained display of most conspicuous brave leadership of the highest order in the face of absolute adversity, Vikram was awarded India's highest decoration in battle, the Param Vir Chakra posthumously.

Through his brave and heroic deed, Vikram brought glory to 13 JAK Rifles and displayed extreme courage and captured the features of Tololing Ridge and Mushkoh Valley.

Vikram was part of the battalion that captured the following peaks:

1. The Hump and Rocky Knob
2. Point 5140
3. Point 4875
4. Area Ledge

A NATION SALUTES

Every duty is holy and devotion to duty is the highest form of worship to God. Help others and you are in heaven.- be selfish and you are in hell.

It was a cruel and an unfathomable sorrow for us. For the world he was a hero, a brave soldier, a brilliant officer and the reason for the country's victory, a true patriot and a martyr. But for us, he was our loving son and a little angel, all of 24. We had dreams for his future, his marriage, his family. We had hoped that Vikram would come back home victorious and we would celebrate his achievements. We would ask him about his missions and he would share stories of his acts of bravery. He would excitedly tell us about what made him go for the operation, how he missed us and how it was our love that drove his passion. We had waited for him and treasured his letters. We had consoled ourselves for it was just a matter of time when we would receive him instead of his letters.

We had hoped that he would come back into our arms, safe and happy. Instead it was Vikram's body that returned and the hope of his voice ringing in our ears and his twinkling bright eyes crashed in a deafening silence.

Vikram was cremated with full military honours. His body was kept in the city ground. Many dignitaries of the state government, representatives of Chief of Army Staff, regiments and unit commanders and nearly 20,000 people joined to pay tribute and bid farewell tp the martyred soul. The ground where his mortal

Former chief minister of Himachal Pradesh Vir Bhadra Singh paying tribute to nation's baraveheart

Prem Kumar Dhumal, the then chief minister of Himachal Pradesh, laying wreath at Vikram's pyre

Param Vir Vikram Batra was cremated with full military honour

remains were kept for all to pay their homage has been renamed as Capt. Vikram Batra Stadium.

Vikram had given up all his dreams, wishes and happiness for the love of his country.

The entire town of Palampur reverberated with the slogans of *Vikram Batra amar rahe.* His pyre was lit by his younger brother Vishal and the Last Post was sounded by Army buglers. The entire city of Palampur remained closed in mourning in Vikram's honour and as a mark of respect.

The Chief of the Army staff, Gen. VP Malik, visited us and told us, 'Had this boy returned from Kargil, he would be sitting in my seat by his retirement.' This was a great honour for OUT beloved son coming from the highest officer of the Indian Army.

Only two days back Vikram had written a letter to his younger brother:

Don't take tension and keep doing your bit faithfully and sincerely. Take life in its stride. You will realize you are the happiest person.

Vikram's gone never to return. He has left behind eternal tears of sorrow, some unfulfilled dreams and wishes, broken hearts, a love lost, a shattered family trying to remain strong, sad yet brave parents, a grieving yet proud brother, some treasured letters, priceless memories, a great sacrifice, an undying name and an inspiring heroic tale of a young officer who led India to its glorious victory.

Maj. Gen. lan Cardozo, in *Param Vir: Our Heroes in Battle,* sums this rekindling of ancient valour succinctly:

> *The Kargil was a war where young of/ leers of the Army were in their 'element'. In no previous wars had young officers dominated the scene as did the young gladiators in Kargil. Amongst (hem were some whose deeds were not recorded at all and, therefore, not recognized. However, from amongst them all the one who captured the imagination of the public most through the media, was young, ever cheerful Capt. Vikram Batra. His bold, courage, patriotic fervour and the daredevil risks he took mission after mission filled the public with wonder and awe. He seemed to be invincible, but every time he sailed forth to meet new challenges and dangers, people prayed for his safe return.*

A SOLDIER'S LOVE STORY

Vikram was a very cheerful person and a magnetic personality. He charmed whoever came in his contact. It was in Chandigarh that he found the girl whom he would have married.

It was in the Department of English (Evening) at Punjab University where Vikram met Dimple and fell in love with her. He had told me about the girl and to ensure his seriousness, I had asked him whether he was sure about it and he had expressed confidence in the relationship.

Vikram and Dimple spent a good two years together in Chandigarh. The bond got stronger as the days of his departure to the academy came closer. Before he went to join the academy, Vikram introduced his twin Vishal to Dimple and told him to meet her whenever he travelled to Chandigarh. Dimple was ecstatic on Vikram's passing out and his final commissioning. Both were waiting for the day when Vikram would be promoted to the rank of captain to tie the knot. Five days before Vikram's martyrdom, Vishal was in Chandigarh. Dimple came to see him at the station. She had mentioned to Vishal then to get them married this time when Vikram returns from the war.

Once, when Vikram was in Palampur on his way back to Sopore after the completion of his training in Mhow (Madhya Pradesh), I was surprised when he suddenly packed his briefcase and got ready to leave for Chandigarh. I asked him the reason of his sudden visit to Chandigarh to which he replied that he had received a telephone call from Dimple. Her parents were getting her engaged to a boy from her community. I told Vikram to let them do so, if they think that would be right for her, to which he immediately replied, 'Papa! How is it possible? We were in a relationship for the last two years and committed to each other.' I again questioned him, 'Are you both sure of your feelings?' He immediately replied 'Definitely Papa.' I said, 'Then go ahead.' The boy who would go on to be a national hero was equally committed to the love of his life in his personal life too.

He went to Chandigarh and came back after a day or so. I was convinced of his sincerity and loyalty to the girl.

When the news of Vikram's demise came, Vishal did not have the courage to speak to her. During the cremation, she came along with her brother and wept quietly. Vikram was the only man she loved. She teaches in a school in Chandigarh and has decided to live with Vikram's memories. We tried to change her mind, but in vain. The cards and gifts given to her by Vikram still adorn her shelf at her home. And Vikram still remains in her heart.

THE CEASEFIRE

Flightened of serious consequences, the Prime Minister of Pakistan prevailed upon America's intervention to persuade India for a ceasefire.

As soon as the Drass sub-sector was cleared of Pakistani forces, the fighting ceased on 26 July 1999. The day has since been marked as Kargil Vijay Diwas in India.

Months after the ceasefire, when the unit of 13 JAK Rifles, posted at Lucknow, was celebrating the Raising Day, we were

Vikram's Battalion receiving the 'Bravest of the Brave' Award after the victory in KargitWar

invited to attend the function. The Unit celebrated their victory and achievement in the Kargil War with full enthusiasm. The Unit had won a rare honour of securing two Param Vir Chakras for Capt. Vikram Batra and Rifleman Sanjay Kumar. The Unit was awarded with the tide 'Bravest of the Brave' by Chief of the Army Staff, Gen. VP Malik.

It was a grand celebration where the present and retired staff of the Unit danced at the time of gala dinner. I too was requested to participate on the dance floor. Two contrasting emotions cruised within me that day: the pain of losing my son and an immense sense of pride for his role in the victory for the country and standing up for her honour. I was choked with mixed emotions. That night I danced with tears in my eyes.

SUPREME HONOUR BECKONS

It was 26 January 2000, the 51st Republic Day ceremony was being celebrated at Rajpath, New Delhi. We were invited to receive the Param Vir Chakra (PVC) on behalf of Capt. Vikram Batra (Posthumously).

I still remember the day when I received the PVC on behalf of my son Capt. Vikram Batra from the president, RK Narayan, in the

Honour galore: Vikram's father, Girdhari Lal Batra, receiving the Param Vir Chakra on Vikram's behalf from the then president, KR Narayanan on 26 January 2000

presence of the prime minister, Atal Bihari Vajpayee, President of Zambia and Vice President of India on stage. It was a proud moment for me. On our way back, after the function, I could not stop myself, and broke down. If Vikram himself would have received the highest gallantry award of the nation, his dreams would have been fulfilled. But destiny had other plans.

Citation

Captain Vikram Batra, Param Vir Chakra (Posthumous)
13 Jammu and Kashmir Rifles (1C 57556)

During 'Operation Vijay', on 20 June 1999, Captain Vikram Batra, Commander Delta Company was tasked to attack Point 5140. Captain Batra with his company skirted around the feature from the East and maintaining surprise reached within assaulting distance of the enemy. Captain Batra reorganized his column and motivated his men to physically assault the enemy position. Leading from the front, he in a daredevil assault, pounced on the enemy and killed four of them in a hand-to-hand fight. On 7 July 1999, in another operation in the area of Point 4875, his company was tasked to clear a narrow feature with sharp cutting on either side and heavily fortified enemy defenses that covered the only approach to it. For speedy operation, Captain Batra assaulted the enemy options along a narrow ridge and engaged the enemy in a fierce hand-to-hand fight and killed five enemy soldiers at point blank range. Despite sustaining grave injuries, he crawled towards the enemy and hurled grenades clearing the position with utter disregard to his personal safety, leading from the front, he rallied his men and pressed on the attack and achieved a near impossible military task in the face of heavy enemy fire. The officer, however, succumbed to his injuries. Inspired by his daredevil act, his troops fell upon the enemy with vengeance, annihilated them and captured Point 4875.

Captain Vikram Batra, thus, displayed the most conspicuous personal bravery and leadership of the highest order in the face of the enemy and made the supreme sacrifice in the highest traditions of the Indian Army.

VIKRAM BATRA: AWARDS AND HONOURS

Military Honours:

- Param Vir Chakra
- Regiment Honour
- Badge of Sacrifice
- Certificate of Honour
- Special Service Medal
- Operation Vijay Medal

Civil Awards

- Veer Savarkar Shaurya Award (National Level, Maharashtra)
- RSS Award
- Himotkarsh National Integration Award (State Level, Himachal Pradesh)
- Himachal Kesari Award (State level, Himachal Pradesh)
- A Shaurya Puraskar, D.A.V. Colleges Management Committee
- Madhya Pradesh Pride Award (Special Award)

IN REMEMBRANCE

Reliving Vikram: A Mother's Memoir

Vikram – the name itself symbolizes valour and bravery. When after the birth of our two daughters, we were blessed with twin sons, we were overjoyed. We always prayed to God to give us a son, but today I understand that He gave us one for the nation and one for us. A follower of Lord Rama, I nicknamed our twin sons Luv and Kush after the twin brave sons of Lord Rama. Later while admitting them in the school we named Luv as Vikram and Kush as Vishal. In Sanskrit, 'Vikram' means an abundance of bravery and he actually proved the worth of his name, its character and its strength. Now we feel, he was bravery incarnate.

Vikram was jovial, sweet natured, softspoken and got along easily with everyone. Vikram had a physical bearing to match his pleasant personality. He excelled in sports, cultural activities and was even a green belt in karate; he was academically sharp and could remember answers to mathemetical numericals during his primary classes. A popular child with a pleasing smile, Vikram was respectful to elders and loving towards youngsters. A colleague of mine once said about Vikram, 'Madam Batra, your son will be a big man some day,' but we had no inkling of the enormity he would eventually achieve.

Vikram was fearless and courageous right from his childhood. Once when a snake crawled into our corridor, I was terrified seeing the reptile and called out for Vikram. He rushed out of his room hearing me shout. Without missing a beat, he took a stick and crushed the snake's head. At moments of crises people tend to get nervous. But not my Vikram!

While he was posted in Sopore in Kahsmir, which was a heavy militancy-prone area, once he had an encounter with militants firing from both sides. A bullet just missed him by a mere fraction. He confided this to his sister when he came to Palampur. He said, 'Didi, perhaps that bullet was not made for me. Maybe there will be some other bullet on which my name will be written.'

Once he called us on telephone from base camp in Brass. I asked him about his well-being. He laughed his unassuming laughter and said, *'Chhake thok rahe hain'* (We are hitting sixers), as if he was not in the battlefield, but a cricket field. I asked, 'Is there no fear to life?' and he replied, 'What fear! Your son is a Loin. He is not born to be afraid. If a bullet would hit me, I shall bear in my chest, not my back.' Such was the fearless fervour of my son.

As a mother I've suffered an irreparable loss, but at the same time I feel proud and honoured for bearing a son who did not flinch from his duty. He made the supreme sacrifice for the protection and integrity of the motherland. He has sanctified my womb and glorified my motherhood.

– Kama! Kanta Batra

Ode to a Son: A Father's Pride

Vedanta philosophy says that every soul is running towards perfection, but my son ran so fast that he went ahead of all of us. He was in a hurry to cross the goal at the earliest.

To sacrifice one's life in the prime of youth, and to achieve martyrdom while protecting one's motherland, is the highest human sacrifice one can make. Martyrs are blessed with the virtues of selfless and true love for their people, their country and humanity at large. I believe it to be a godly instinct.

Holy scriptures say that the ultimate goal of human life is nirvana or moksha. Lord Krishna said in the *Bhagavad Gita* that whosoever sacrifices his life in the battlefield for the establishment of truth and righteousness directly comes to me and achieves liberation (moksha).

हतो वा प्राप्स्यसि स्वर्ग, जित्वा वा भोक्ष्यसे महीम्।
तस्मादुत्तिष्ठ कौन्तेय युद्धाय कृतनिश्चयः।।
Slain thou shall win heaven,
Victorious thou shall enjoy the earth;
Therefore arise, O son of Kunti,
Resolved upon battle.

Martyrs are part incarnation of gods and graced with godly virtues. They are always prepared for the supreme sacrifice. What better way to serve the nation than to sacrifice one's life for the motherland and its people.

यदृच्छया चोपन्नं स्वर्गद्वारामपावृतम् ।
सुखिनः क्षत्रियाः पार्थ लभन्ते युद्धमीदृशम् ।।
Happy indeed are the Kshatrias, o Partha,
Who are called to fight in such a battle
That comes of itself as an open door to heaven.

People like Vikram are neither born nor do they die; they come and go after performing their duties. Such people are assigned to perform specific tasks by the supreme power. They are the spark of the eternal light that glitters for a while and vanish, just to enlighten the right path and leave behind the memories and imprints of their good deeds and extraordinary feats to follow.

Apart from being a father, I have observed Vikram keenly as a teacher and found him totally different. He had a heavenly glow on his face since childhood. Vikram was brilliant and signs of his doing something extraordinary were visible since then. He has proved as a worthy son, who has given us honour and pride and made our life worthy. Thousands of salutations to him. He is always with us.

– GL Batra

A Bond Sublime: Brothers Forever

Our journey started in a small town, Palampur, in the Dhauladhar ranges in Kangra district of Himachal Pradesh.

Luv, as we called Vikram, and I, Kush, his identical twin (14 minutes younger), had a life full of laughter and pranks till we grew up and decided that we wanted to be part of the Indian Armed Forces.

How fast times flies. And how all of us don't get what we want. Luv made it to the Indian Military Academy in March 1996 and I, rejected thrice by the Service Selection Board, had to settle for a career in management.

When Vikram visited us during his annual leave, looking tall and handsome in his uniform, I realized how much passion I still had for the armed forces. With great pride in my eyes, I watched my brother marching ahead in life so much faster than we had imagined.

Having got commissioned into 13 JAK Rifles with his first posting in Sopore, Vikram already had some daring face-to-face combat with the enemy in insurgency operations. We knew he was born to fight against all odds.

It was around the same time that the Kargil War happened and he was asked to move there to help fellow soldiers flush out Pakistani intruders who had entered the Indian terrain. The last call

Vikram made to Mom and Dad on his movement had given us some jitters, but we always knew that he was a daring officer for whom facing any challenge was a cakewalk.

His last statement to one of our friends before proceeding to Kargil that 'Either I would hoist the Tricolour or come back wrapped in it' still echoes in our hearts. It showed what iron he was made of.

It's been 17 years now. A lot has changed and a lot has remained the same. I have many more grey strands in my hair. Vikram remains as youthful as ever. Time cannot touch him. In all these years, there has hardly been a day in the family that passed by without a mention of Vikram.

The greatest memory etched in my" heart so deep is from way back in 1985 when Doordarshan telecasted the serial *Param Vir Chakra.* We didn't have a TV then and would watch it at our neighbour's house. I could never have imagined even in my wildest dreams that the stories we saw in this popular serial would one day become so real for us. Vikram caught the fancy of millions of Indians - and still continues to remain in their thoughts.

Many a time strangers come up to me and tell me that I look like Vikram or ask if they have seen me somewhere. I have been asked by hundreds of people if I am related to Vikram. And each time I'm little more proud to be Vikram's doppelganger, not to mention to be his sibling.

I would dream that one day Vikram would rise to the rank of a brigadier or even higher and then I would walk by his side as a proud brother. Today he's no more, but I've lost count of exactly how many times Vikram has made me proud of him. Once when I signed my name in a hotel register in London, an Indian standing nearby read my name and asked, 'Do you know Vikram Batra?' Is there any better reward than the fact that people recognize Vikram even in far off London?

Yes, death is the ultimate truth of life but how many of us have the courage to face death with open arms? My brother Vikram was a Param Vir Bravest of the Brave.

My dream of visiting Vikram as a commanding officer of a regiment couldn't come true. But he still commands the hearts of the soldiers posted in Kargil and Brass.

When I talk about Luv, I don't know where to begin. Ours was a childhood spent in the hills of Palampur, making the most of our identical looks – playing pranks, filling in for each other and at times even getting punished for one another's mistakes. The similarity ran deeper than looks. We also had the same interests. Both of us started playing table tennis at the age of 10. It's another story that Vikram went on to become the school champion for five consecutive years. But I'd like to believe that I had a big hand in that. After all, I chose to lose to him in the semi-finals in the fifth year so that he could make the school record. But deep in my heart, I know that my brother - Sher Shah of Kargil was a winner right from the start.

'Sher Shah of Kargil' – that's what the enemy too called Vikram. That's the mark he made on them on those unforgiving mountains of Kargil. I don't know at what stage Vikram marched way ahead of all of us. We'd grown up as regular kids, making our choices as we went along. The first different choice that I remember is when our father started giving us ₹50 a month for the school bus fare. I chose to travel to school by bus. Vikram opted to walk it and instead spent that money in the canteen. As we grew up, Vikram opted for the army, and I eventually settled for business administration. How thrilled he was when he made it to the IMA, Dehradun.

It was 6 December 1997 when Vikram's dream came true. He took the oath as an officer of the Indian Army. Mom and Dad pinned up the stars on his shoulder. He stood there smiling from ear to ear in his crew cut and several kilos thinner after the rigorous training. It was a grand moment. But it wasn't going to be an easy life and Vikram knew that.

When he'd come home on annual leave, we would talk for hours about the challenges he faced in Sopore, which was his first posting. He had been commissioned into 13 JAK Rifles. We would dream of the day he would command his regiment and I would get a chance to attend some of the regimental functions with his family and children. That dream is lost now.

Vikram was awarded the country's highest gallantry award, posthumously. He was only 24. His famous words *Yeh dil maange more,* after victory over the enemy, still ring in my ears.

I had longed to visit those mountains that he conquered. Years later when I got a call from NDTV as part of a decade celebration of Vijay Diwas they were doing on Vikram (though I had already booked my tickets with Dad for 24 July 2009 wherein we both were to join the Vijay Diwas celebration at Drass), there was no second thoughts. It was as if Vikram was calling me to have a chat with him. I didn't look back, and packed my bags and set out to the mountains. I landed in Leh at 10.30 in the morning, five days before Vikram's tenth death anniversary.

The Valley is more beautiful than it is made to appear in the books. From the snow-capped hills surrounding it, I could almost sense Vikram looking at me. I then began the road trip to Drass to meet him. The mountain wind blew faster than the speed of the car and in my mind there was just one picture - of the bearded young man who had become a legend for pushing the enemy back at insurmountable heights where even life does not exist.

A little outside Leh, we reached Gurudwara Pathar Sahib. I said a prayer for Vikram and for all those great soldiers guarding those mountains and our motherland. I recalled what Vikram had written in one of his last letters before the attack:

Life is at total risk. Anything can happen here. Take care of yourself and Mom and Dad... My picture has appeared in The Times of India. Keep a copy for me. I want to see it once I'm back.

The picture had appeared on the front page of *The Times of India* on 2 July 1999. It showed him standing with an anti-aircraft gun and weapons he had seized from the Pakistani soldiers. This was after the first ferocious attack on Peak 5140 launched after they performed *puja* at the Ghumri Base Gamp with the call of *Durga Mata ki Jai.*

Vikram and his men captured Point 5140 on 20 June 1999, and two weeks later, when his company launched the attack on Point 4875 on 7 July, Vikram was fatally wounded — hit by sniper fire. The company captured the peak, but after 11 casualties. Vikram was one of them.

It was months later, at the Western Command Headquarters, that I met the junior commissioned officer (JCO) who was with Vikram the day he was fatally wounded. He was the last man to speak with Vikram. Sub. Maj. Raghunath Singh started wailing when he saw me. He solved the mystery of my twin's death for me: A young officer, Vikram's junior, was hit and crying for help. The JCO wanted to go out to help but Vikram stopped him. 'The enemy was firing heavily. "You have a family and children back home, I will do this," sahib said. He stopped me with these words and went out,' Raghunath Singh told me as he wept inconsolably. When Vikram was hit by sniper fire, the charged company went berserk, mad with rage at their leader being hit, and killed the enemy soldiers. The Tricolour was planted atop Point 4875 - they call it Batra Top now.

Vikram's body reached Palampur before the sun rose on 11 July 1999. He was wrapped in the Tricolour, lying calm almost as if he was trying to catch up on sleep that he had lost during these arduous assaults on those treacherous peaks.

Was I really so close to those peaks that I could almost see him fighting there? I wanted to reach up there as fast as possible, but the track was treacherous - the rocky mountain on one side and the sheer fall on the other. In some time, we had left the Indus River behind.

It was a breathtaking journey. A place so beautiful and yet caught in the crossfire of war a decade ago. Midway, at one of the military posts, we had lunch with the commanding officer of 4 JAK Rifles. I also met an officer six months senior to Vikram - now a major – and a JCO, both of whom had fought the war together with Vikram. 'You look so much like Vikram Sir,' the JCO said and hugged me. I've been told that a billion times in the last 10 years. There are people now who know me a? Captain Vikram Batra's brother. Many of them even walk into my office and stare at me as if they know me. Some of them even say, 'We've seen you somewhere.' When I tell them I'm Captain Batra's twin, they say, 'Oh, *Yeh dil maange more',* and shake my hand.

'Call of duty' – the mention of these words takes me back to the days he was to be commissioned as an officer. When he was in the IMA, the footnote of Vikram's letterpad read, 'If Death comes to me before I prove my blood, I promise I'll kill Death.' You kept your word, Vikram. My brother, my twin, I salute you.

– Vishal Batra

A Prankster-Charmer: A Sister Recollects

Table tennis was like something that had got into the blood of both the twins, Vikram and Vishal. There was a clear directive from dad to both to split the time between studies and sports, and sticking to the discipline was never easy... they had their own dreams of representing their school in the nationals after all. Vikram was always the naughtier one and Vishal more submissive.

While Vishal was always back home on time, Vikram was invariably late and then tried to sneak into the house. The window of our room was pretty large and was next to the main gate of the house. Vikram would knock on the window and ask me to open the drawing room door silently. I used to check and make sure Dad was not around and then open the door for him. He would silently enter the house by taking his shoes off and going to his bed straightaway. I had just returned home at Mandi from Amritsar after visiting some of my relatives there. I was not aware of the incursions at Kargil when all of a sudden I got a call from Vikram, who assumed that I would be aware of the Kargil news. Vikram in his haste to tell me the news said, 'Main uparja raha hun.' (What he meant to say was 'I'm going to the top.' But I, in my panic, assumed that Vikram uttered something along the lines of 'I am done with my life!'). For a moment I was taken aback but then he explained that he had got the orders to move to Kargil to fight off the Pakistani infiltrators. I blessed him with a long life but somewhere deep in my heart that sentence kept hitting me hard. I became restless and it kept bothering me till the time battle was on.

As the war continued, I would cry hearing any patriotic song. I was five-month pregnant, when I got the news of his martyrdom. There was no one with Mom and Dad at Palampur, as both Vishal and Nutan were in Delhi. I was the first to reach Palampur to be with them. In between all the developments, I also had a miscarriage, though I was blessed with a baby boy three years later.

***

The boy always surprised us. Back in 1997, when our younger sister Nutan was getting married, we had almost given up hope that Vikram would be able to make it for the wedding on February 12, which also happened to be Nutan's birthday, as he had recently joined the academy. But Vikram being Vikram, he made it just in time to be a part of the celebration. Apparently he got special permission from his senior to attend the function back home. He definitely had his way with people. Such a charmer my brother was!

– Seema Sethi

A Brother Keeps His Promise: A Sister's Tribute

My childhood memories are dotted with happy moments shared with my siblings, not to mention Vikram. He was very loving and always tried to make me feel special with his small but significant gestures. He used to lovingly call me 'Munia', and even though I was a year-and-a-half older than him, my kid brother was particularly careful about fulfilling smallest of my wishes.

When I sit back and recall, umpteen moments come to my mind – and every moment says something special about Vikram. I remember, we had a club in Palampur, which had indoor and outdoor sports facilities. Vikram and Vishal were regulars there and used to win many awards for table tennis. Once I expressed my keenness to Vikram to try my hand at the game, but since the place was dominated by boys, I was a little sceptical in going there. Vikram promised me that he will do something about it. Next day, to everyone's surprise, I saw him bringing the TT table home after taking permission from the caretaker, since the club was closing for a few days for Diwali holidays. The table stayed at our home for the next three to four days and Vikram made sure that I got to play the game as much as I wanted.

When I asked him why he went overboard while I just casually mentioned about playing the game, he said in his characteristic style, 'Munia, I am a man of words.' Indeed he was; it was only a matter of time when the whole world would witness how Vikram put his duty before himself during the Kargil War.

My visit to Indian Military Academy in Dehradun to attend Vikram's passing out parade with my husband, when I was newly married, was the most memorable event of my life. There was something about Vikram that made him stand out amongst all the gentlemen cadets. He was looking dashing in the army olives. The joy on his face was unmistakable, and so were the tears in my eyes, because he had never let me cry before.

Even as a passing out gentleman cadet, he made sure that all his friends and family members who had come to attend the ceremony got an opportunity to explore the amazing campuses of IMA and the Forest Research Institute in Dehradun.

He had a way to get things done, using his charm, wit and simplicity. I wish he had survived the war. India would have witnessed many more stories of valour and commitment from this son of the motherland.

Long Live Vikram Batra!

– Nutan Malik

Till We Meet Again: Jaani

joined D.A.V. College, Chandigarh, in July 1992. As I moved towards the hostel, my eyes were drawn to two young men who were approaching from the opposite direction. There was something eyecatching about both of them; they exuded a comfortable confidence and had a pleasant demeanour. But it was something else that had caught my attention - both looked identical. The only thing that differentiated them was that one wore specs and the other had a mole on his nose. 'Hi, I'm Hardeep Sandhu, friends call me Nippy,' I said. Tm Batra - Vikram Batra,' said one of the young men. I don't know why, but to me it resonated of the introduction of Bond -James Bond. 'This is my brother Vishal; friends call us Luv and Kush,' he continued. These simple greetings were the start of a timeless friendship.

College started; classes were till about 2 p.m. Vikram, I found, did everything with enthusiasm and put his heart and soul into it. He got his books issued in time, was up and about early in the morning, had breakfast and attended all (well, almost all) the classes. I used to get up by about 1 p.m. and used to be at the hostel canteen waiting for Vikram and Vishal for lunch after they had attended their classes. Vikram would ask, 'Why don't you attend the classes?' I used to simply laugh and say, 'Jaani, everything that is taught is in the books and as far as the attendance issue is concerned, well I have the entire year to take care of that.' Thereafter Vikram, or 'Jaani' as I use to lovingly call him, used to go for table tennis or athletics practice for the oncoming college events. He often tried to motivate me to try at some of the events and activities, and I used to reply with a grin, 'You are doing it, I am doing it, it's one and the same thing.' Evenings used to find us at the *geri* (going somewhere in coloquilal Punjabi) route between Sector 10 and 11 of Chandigarh or at Sector 17 market and at times at the 'lovers' lane' behind Government College of Girls (GCG), Chandigarh.

Sundays were booked for a movie at KG Theatre of Sector 17, which used to cost ₹7.50 at that time and then at the local fast food joint Hot Millions, popularly known as HMs. Those were the good times.

Vikram, I found, was one of the most popular guys in the hostel and the college. He was helpful, would go out of his way for any friend who needed him, always smiling and jovial, with a mischievous twinkle in his eyes. I never failed to notice that he knew everybody and everyone knew him. I had given the entrance exam for National Defence Academy (NDA), Khadakwasla earlier and had also undergone the Service Selection Board (SSB). One day Vikram came to my room in the hostel and said, 'Hey, the NDA results are out - let's go and check it out.' I went along with him to a cyber cafe in Sector 11.1 could see that he was more excited than I was. He was a diehard^w/i. Joining the Indian Army was his only dream. After scanning the paper for some time he let out a whoop of joy and shouted, Jaani! You've got through and not only have you got through, you've come third in all-India merit.' The following days were spent in celebration and partying. Thereafter, we went shopping for the list of items to be brought when I joined NDA. I still remember the gleam in his eyes while we ticked each item off the list and after the initial euphoria wore off, on a serious note I asked Vikram when he planned to join the Army. He replied that he had to prepare and train himself before he became a part of the elite Armed Forces. He then went into another world telling me his plans to join the NCC at college and then appearing for the Combined Defence Services (CDS) exam after college, then he added 'Yeah, there is one more aim: 'Live Life King Size'.' I smiled and told him that he already was more than ready to join the Army. In December 1992, I joined NDA and Vikram continued his college. We were constantly in touch on phone and letters. When I got my first term break in June 1993, he told me that his college would also close for summer. I was disappointed as it meant that he would be off to his hometown at Palampur and I might not get an opportunity to meet him. He laid my apprehension to rest by saying that he had planned to spend part of his leave at Palampur and Mandi and the rest at Chandigarh so that we could 'freak out'. That became the norm after that - after every six months when I was on my term break - Vikram would spend part of his time at Chandigarh. He would be all excited and would prod me for each and every detail of the training at NDA and then replicating the same. We used to drive to Palampur in my dad's car to Vikram's parents and then to Mandi, lazing in the sun at Neugal Cafe at Palampur, going to Timber Trail, trips to Kasauli, Nahan and Pinjore. My parents knew that our trips were always at the drop of a hat, and whenever my parents wanted to advise me on something, they would ask Vikram to convey it to me saying that 'Nippy will only listen to you.' That was fact. I could not refuse him anything and neither could he to me. In all the years we spent together, we never had a single argument, except that one instance when we both were certain that the other had had a peg too much and wanted to 'safely' drive the car. How I used to look forward to those twenty days of term break: 'Days Left To Go Home' (DLTGH) a common expression in Academy lingo.

Vikram was doing extremely well in college and also at NCC. He had also bagged the best-cadet award. Then the day we all had been eagerly waiting for came - the CDS results were out and Jaani, obviously made through. At that time, I was in the third term of Indian Military Academy (IMA), Dehradun. A large number of Gentlemen Cadets at IMA already knew that Sandhu's brother was joining the Academy. I waited for his arrival at IMA and the Company he would be allotted. He was to join Jessore Company while I was Senior Under Officer (SUO) Sangro. Vikram was on the top of the world; so was I. We used to meet often depending on the training schedule. Wednesday were movie days and most of the gentlemen cadets used to undergo 'strengthening exercises' before the movie. Vikram used to be called out by me so that he could enjoy the movie with 'appointment privileges'. After the initial few times, Vikram told me that since his company was undergoing the 'strengthening exercises', he would like to be with them. I looked at him and was happy at his answer; he was a team player who would stand by his team at all times. I let him join his company and then instructed the Appointment who was showing particular interest in them to let Jessore Company move in to the Khetarpal Auditorium for the movie. As Vikram moved in he told me, 'You don't give up, do you?' and then he added, 'When the going gets tough, the tough get going.' Though he had to undergo the one-and-a-half year of training at IMA, I knew that he was already ready to shoulder more responsibilities. As expected, he completed his training with flying colours.

On his commissioning in December 1997,1 had taken leave from my unit and was at IMA to celebrate the big day. I had promised him that I would come on my bike. He had been commissioned into 13 JAK Rifles. I asked Vikram, 'Now, you're happy, you've realized your dream.' He pleasantly surprised me with his reply, 'No, not yet, I'm born for greater things.' So true buddy, so true! Vikram and I rode back from Dehradun to Chandigarh on my Bullet (Enfield 350) bike singing *Yeh dosti hum nahi chhoddenge,* while my parents followed in their car behind. Once our leaves finished, we both joined back our respective units - he was in the North and I in the North East. Our leaves used to be planned together so that we could meet, either at Chandigarh or at Palampur. We used to talk about our experiences in our units and give pearls of wisdom to each other on the various issues faced. When Vikram had to go for the Commando Course, I along with his brother Vishal went to the station to see him off, helping in the loading of hisfauji trunk. He was in his element, looking forward to the course and meeting all his course mates who were boarding from Delhi.

We were both enjoying the Army life and happy with the way things were shaping up when the Kargil War happened. He was deployed in the thick of things and I was in touch with him through letters. On 20 June, when he was part of the team that captured Tololing, he said 'Jaani, your birthday present, Totaling Heights'. He was full of excitement and in his spirited manner said, 'When you go home, tell them of us and say, for your tomorrow, we gave our today.' I told him that I have been watching him on news and asked him to just take care of himself, as unlike video games there won't be three chances.

I was the Aide-de-Camp (ADC) to a Corps Commander in the North East when I got a call in the middle of the night from a course mate 'Sandhu, Vikram has made the supreme sacrifice.' I just sat down and put the receiver back. I was crying the entire night packing my bags to go to Palampur. The next day I informed the Corps Commander and requested to be allowed to proceed on leave. Vikram's brother, Vishal, called me and said that they were all waiting for me to reach Palampur to perform the last rites. I told him that it would take me two days to reach the nearest airport at Guwahati and another day to reach Palampur and asked him not to keep the hero waiting. I reached Palampur when everyone was getting back from the cremation ground. Entire Palampur was there. I met Vikram's parents and Vishal and just hugged them; I didn't say anything, there was nothing to be said. The next day Vishal, I and their maternal uncle took the ashes and moved to Haridwar. En-route the car developed a snag and I said, 'It's like old times, Vikram, Vishal and Nippy are together and in trouble again.' Vishal said 'Jaani doesn't want to leave us' and I told him he never will.

It has been stated that energy can neither be created nor destroyed; it can only be transformed from one form to another. The energy of the human body is the same, what is that form that it transforms into is something which we are not aware of. A person who is in your heart can never be away from you as he is within you. Physical presence is replaced by memories, which cannot be taken away from you.

He has been Vikram, Luv, Sher Shah, a friend, a son, a brother and a hero for the nation but for me he has and will always be my Jaani. Till we meet again, Jaani.

– Lt Col Hardeep Sandhu (Retd), Vikram's Friend

Barkha Dutf Narrates: Chronicals from Kargil

I can never forget Vikram Batra's smile. It travelled from a wide-set jaw right up to his gleaming eyes that shone with courage and the satisfaction of a job well done. His was one of the earliest interviews I did at the frontline of the Kargil War between India and Pakistan in 1999; his would also be the first obituary I would write.

I didn't know when I first met him. We were sitting huddled together in the shelter of a soft white tent at the base camp in Ghumri; Vikram and his men had just come down to the foothills from the hostile, jagged mountain peaks after successfully reclaiming Point 5140 from the entrenched Pakistani infiltrators. But Vikram wore his courage lightly. You couldn't sense any anxiety, fatigue or apprehension in him; on the contrary he and his boys were sitting around in a friendly huddle, flipping through the pages of a faded Cosmopolitan magazine - an incongruous image for a war. But that was Vikram zinda-dil, fearless and brimming with youthful bravado and enthusiasm. He was appropriately code-named 'Sher Shah' after the 'Lion King' celebrated in medieval Indian history. His thick beard and smiling eyes camouflaged the fact that he was still so young - barely 24 - a couple of years younger than I was at the time we met. He spoke of the ordeal of battle as if it were just another day at the office, the matter-of-fact modesty in fact reinforcing how extraordinarily brave he was.

As Vikram and his fellow soldiers had moved up the eastern flank of Point 5140 (which until now dominated the town of Brass and allowed the Pakistanis direct aim at Indian targets), they came under heavy fire. But they had to keep moving. 'If we had stopped at any point, we would have become the target,' Vikram told me, 'there was no looking back.' At one point the Pakistanis interrupted the radio frequency Vikram and his men were using and bellowed out a warning. 'Sher Shah, don't come up, we will teach you a lesson.' The threat made Vikram even more determined. The peak was reclaimed without any fatalities. It was a watershed moment in the war; Indian helicopters were finally able to fly freely over Drass. My reporting of the war sought to go beyond the battles and tell the individual stories of young heroes like Vikram. I wanted to know them as people; didn't they ever feel scared? How did they deal with fear and loss? I wanted people to understand that there was no contradiction between valour and vulnerability. But among the many soldiers I met, this swashbuckling Captain was unique. When I asked him these questions, he threw his head back and laughed out loud; *Yeh dil maange more,* he told me with a toothy grin, elevating what was till then a Pepsi sales jingle to the status of a national motto. With that single, pithy comment - delivered with a broad smile on his face - Vikram became the face of the Kargil War, just days before he died trying to save the life of a fellow soldier. Later we would get to know that as he jumped to place himself in the line of fire, he told his mate that since he had children he should let Vikram take the hit. That's the sort of man Vikram was.

That night when the TV presenter in the Delhi headquarters read out the news that Vikram was no more, his voice choked; he wasn't able to complete the sentence. Up in the mountains, I struggled through tears to write a befitting farewell; what stayed with me – and does till this day – was his smile. His optimism was contagious, inspiring and full of hope.

Before leaving his ageing parents, Vikram had told them that he would either unfurl the Indian flag to mark victory or come back home draped in one. He did both.

His twin brother Vishal – an eerily spitting image of Vikram – told me that was the instant – as Vikram's body was lifted out of the coffin to be placed on the pyre and the national flag handed over to his family – when he ceased to be intimidated by the spectre of Death. 'You know, when we took him for his final rites, the body was taken from the coffin and the tricolor was handed to Mom. I was holding his body in my hands; it was the first cremation of my life. But at that very moment whatever fear I had of Death went away.'

Vishal (a private banker, who once thought of becoming a soldier) and I were sitting together under the vast expanse of a clear blue sky, staring out at Batra Top - the mountain feature now named after his twin brother. It was Vishal's first trip to Kargil; we had travelled up to the mountains together 10 years after the war. There, in the shelter of the mountains where his brother had been slain, he felt as I did - that he could hear us. Quietly, Vishal allowed himself the tears that he had held back all these years: Then in the shadow of the peak named after his brother, he sat and wrote him a letter, wanting him to know that memories of their shared childhood – the twins had been called Luv and Kush – is what gave him the strength to keep going. He read the letter out loud as if Vikram was right there, looking down at him from a serene white cloud. After that, he stood in wordless salute and allowed the wind to lift the letter to the skies.

We hugged each other and made our way down. Vikram would be a memory that would remain etched in my heart, filling me with a strange mix of tears and pride, every time I thought of him.

We will never forget you, Vikram. You taught me what honour means. You exemplified it.

– Barkha Dutt, Journalist and Columnist

People's Hero: Phraises from Far and Wide

It was only after Vikram's martyrdom that we realized the many ways in which this simple lad from Palampur touched so many lives, young and old, near and far.

An army officer of the rank of Lt Gen., while sitting on Vijay Diwas function at Brass, once told me that Vikram was not just an army officer; he was a true country lover and was above the awards. If there would have been an award higher than PVG, he would have got it.

The principal of his school wrote in his letter that though everybody takes birth and everybody dies, but the way Vikram went nobody did that way.

An NRI from the US wrote that his wife was expecting a baby for the first time and he was so inspired by Vikram that he had decided if he is blessed with a son, then he will name him after Vikram.

In a letter a young man wrote that he keeps a photograph of Vikram in his wallet and whenever he is frustrated, he sees the photograph to overcome his frustration and he gets inspired.

Chairman of Pepsico India Ltd. wrote that Vikram has immortalized their commercial slogan *Yeh dil maange more* by quoting it in the battlefield.

An industrialist wrote that he wept only at the time of his mother's death for the first time and it was the second time that he wept on Vikram's passing away. As soon as he heard the news of his death on TV he kept listening to his story constantly for two days.

When Abhishek Bachchan, the actor, met Vikram's twin brother, Vishal, in connection with the film LOG: Kargil being made by the film director JP Dutta, he told Vishal that they are just screen heroes, but Vikram Batra is a real-life hero.

Barkha Dutt, the well-known TV journalist, on meeting us at Rashtrapati Bhavan in New Delhi on the evening of a Republic Day party said that Vikram was very enthusiastic and cheerful when she met him after the capture of Point 5140 at the base camp in Drass. She had a cup of tea with him, and interviewed him, where he showed her the anti-aircraft gun and other weapons captured from the enemy.

Her eyes welled up with tears as she remembered the impact of Capt. Vikram Barta's (PVC) message of victory 'When he said *Yeh dil maange more.* TV carried the impact of his words. When he died a week later, we were flooded with letters and calls from people who wanted to get in touch with his family.'

In her book This Unquiet Land Barkha has described Capt. Vikram Batra in her own way:

'The heroism that (Capt.) Vikram and other soldiers who fought in Kargil displayed was perhaps most famously brought into the living rooms of their fellow Indians by Vikram Batra, a soldier with 13 Jammu and Kashmir Rifles. I met him at the base camp in Ghumri in the early days of the war. This was my first major interview with a soldier on the front line. His would also be the first obituary I would write. His men and he had just returned from a successful operation and were trading tales around a shared dog-eared copy of *Cosmopolitan* in a faded white tent that looked like a tiny snowdrop against the green and brown expanse of the mountains. His smiling eyes framed by a thick beard, Vikram was rather appropriately code-named "Sher Shah" - after the sixteenth-century "Lion King" eulogized in medieval Indian history. As he casually flipped through the pages of the magazine, which seemed oddly out of place in this setting, he recounted the details of his latest operation with the enthusiasm and bravado of a teenager. As he and his soldiers moved up the eastern flank of Point 5140, the highest mountain peak dominating the town of Drass (thus allowing the Pakistanis direct observation of Indian targets), they came under fierce artillery and small arms fire. The enemy troops were constantly firing illumination rounds to break the cover of darkness under which Vikram's team was moving up. "If we had stopped at any point", Vikram told me, "we would have become the target. There was no looking back." At one point the Pakistanis intercepted the radio frequency being used by the Indians and addressed him by his military code name. They said: "Sher Shah, don't try and come up; you will have a tough time." The challenge boomeranged on the Pakistanis and made Vikram even more determined to rout them. The peak was reclaimed without any fatalities. Indian helicopters were finally able to fly freely over Drass. It was a critical turning point in the war. All of twenty-four, Vikram wore his courage lightly, throwing back his head in uproarious laughter when I questioned him on fear and vulnerability. *Yeh dil maange more,* he told me with a toothy grin - borrowing from the lines of what was till then only a popular Pepsi jingle. In that instant, Vikram Batra became the face of India's self-worth. His contagious optimism immortalized him as the face of Kargil just days before he would die, trying to save a fellow soldier who had come under enemy fire. Much later, his ageing parents would share his last words as he left for the front. Vikram had told them that he would either unfurl the Indian flag to mark victory or come back home draped in one.'

Major JS Punia of 17 Jat Regiment, who had heard Vikram shouting at the enemy, said 'He was the man who would volunteer for the most difficult task. He further elaborated that Capt. Batra and his men were now at a height of more than 16,000 feet and the freezing air made the going more strenuous. They climbed higher towards the ledge; neutralizing whatever resistance they came across. By dawn they had reached the ledge. Vikram could see rifles and the artilleries of the enemy men and he could not hold back his anger. With a fierce battle cry he sprang up and charged followed closely by his men. Within seconds they were grappling with the enemy soldiers in a hand-to-hand combat. Firing filled the air as bayonets flashed and bodies fell to the ground as the battle intensified. Within minutes seven Pakistanis lay dead; their bodies sprawled awkwardly over the jagged rocks on the hill side.'

Captain Naveen Anabru of 13 JAK Rifles, who was rescued by Vikram, remembered him as the livewire during the fighting for Point 4875, in the Mushkoh Valley, living into the bunker for a while and then out again.

जनरल वी पी मलिक

General V P Malik
PVSM, AVSM, ADC

सेना मुख्यालय
नई दिल्ली - 110 011

ARMY HEADQUARTERS
NEW DELHI - 110 011

12821/33/OPR/99/Org 3 (d)

16 Jul 99

Dear Shri Batra,

1. It is with deep sorrow and sympathy that I write to express my condolences, and that of all ranks of the Army, on the sad and untimely demise of your son Capt Vikram Batra. In his death, the Army has lost a dedicated and devoted officer.

2. May God give you the strength to bear the irreparable loss. We share your grief and will always be ready to be of any assistance.

It is a personal loss to me.

With Regards

Yours Sincerely

VP Malik

Shri GL Batra
295, W-5, Near Parking Stand
Palampur
Distt: Kangra
HP – 176 061

एयर चीफ मार्शल अ य टिपणीस

Air Chief Marshal A Y Tipnis
PVSM AVSM VM ADC

वायु सेना मुख्यालय
नई दिल्ली-११००११

Air Headquarters
New Delhi-110011

Air HQ/15028/5/CAS 26 *Jul 99*

Dear Shri Batra,

1. I deeply regret the demise of your valiant son during operations in Kargil Sector. True to the glorious traditions of the Indian Army, Vikram made the supreme sacrifice in the defence of our Motherland. I, along with all personnel of the IAF, salute him for his patriotism and devotion to duty.

2. In this hour of profound grief, we offer our deepest condolences to you and to all other members of your family. We salute a brave family in recognition of Vikram's valiant service.

3. We pray to the Almighty to give you and your family the strength to bear this irreparable loss.

With profound sympathy,

Yours-in-grief,

Anil Tipnis

Shri GL Batra
295/ W-5, Near Parking Stand
Palampur - 176 061
Dist Kangra (HP)

सत्यमेव जयते

राम नाईक

मंत्री
पेट्रोलियम एवं प्राकृतिक गैस
भारत सरकार
नई दिल्ली-110 001

अर्द्ध स.प.संख्या-पी-19018/49/99-आई.ओ.सी/एफ-213

दिसंबर 17, 1999

महोदय,

स्वर्गीय कैप्टन विक्रम बत्रा ने कारगिल युद्ध के दौरान राष्ट्र की सुरक्षा के लिए अपना जीवन न्यौछावर कर सम्पूर्ण राष्ट्र को गौरवान्वित किया ।

2. मुझे यह अहसास है कि स्वयं आपको तथा आपके परिवार को जो क्षति हुई है, उसे भर पाना असंभव है । फिर भी राष्ट्र स्वर्गीय कैप्टन विक्रम बत्रा के बलिदान को ध्यान में रखते हुए आपको पालमपुर में रिटेल आउटलेट डीलरशिप आवंटित करता है । मेरा अनुरोध है कि आप इसे स्वीकार कर हमें अनुग्रहित करने की कृपा करें ।

3. मैं स्वर्गीय कैप्टन विक्रम बत्रा के बलिदान को नमन करता हूँ ।

सादर,

भवदीय,

(राम नाईक)

श्री जी.एल.बत्रा
पिता स्व.कैप्टन विक्रम बत्रा,
मकान नं. 295, वार्ड नं. 5,
नजदीक पार्किंग स्टैण्ड,
पोस्ट- पालमपुर,
जिला कांगड़ा-176061,
हिमाचल प्रदेश ।

दिल्ली कार्यालय : 201-ए शास्त्री भवन, नई दिल्ली-110 001 दूरभाष : 011-338 14 62, 338 66 22 फैक्स : 011-338 61 18
निवास : 9 तीन मूर्ति मार्ग, नई दिल्ली-110 011 दूरभाष : 011-301 71 11, 379 30 80 फैक्स : 011-301 71 12
मुंबई कार्यालय : बुकिंग कार्यालय के पीछे, गोरेगांव रेलवे स्टेशन (पूर्व), मुंबई-400 063 दूरभाष : 022-873 33 39, 873 23 33 फैक्स : 022-873 11 33
निवास : 9 शिवस्मृति, 51 जयप्रकाश नगर, गोरेगांव पूर्व, मुंबई-400 063 दूरभाष : 022-873 03 33 फैक्स : 022-876 63 33

कार्मिक, लोक शिकायत तथा
पेंशन राज्य मंत्री
भारत

VASUNDHARA RAJE

MINISTER OF STATE FOR
PERSONNEL, PUBLIC GRIEVANCES & PENSIONS
INDIA

Shri Batra

The brave deeds of Late Late Capt. Vikram Batra, in recognition of which, he has been conferred with the 'Param Vir Chakra', posthumously, have brought honour to the country.

I wish all the other members of Late Capt. Vikram Batra's family all the very best in life.

Yours sincerely,

Vasundhara Raje

(Vasundhara Raje)

Shri G. L. Batra
H. No. 295, W-5
Palampur
District Kangra
Himachal Pradesh

रक्षा मंत्री, भारत
MINISTER OF DEFENCE
INDIA

July , 1999

Dear Mr Batra,

I write to express my deep sympathy and condolences on my own behalf and on behalf of all ranks in the Army, on the sad and untimely demise of your son IC- 57156H Capt. Vikram Batra on July 07, 1999.

He made the ultimate sacrifice at the altar of duty as a true soldier.

I hope you will bear this loss with courage and fortitude.

With regards,

Yours sincerely,

George Fernandes

Shri GL Batra
295, W - 5,
Near Parking Stand, Palam Pur,
Distt. - Kangra
State - Himachal Pradesh
Pin- 176061

ले. जनरल आर के साहनी, पी वी एस एम, ए वी एस एम
सैनिक आसूचना महानिदेशक
Lt Gen R K Sawhney, PVSM, AVSM
Director General Military Intelligence
Tele : 3011618

सैनिक आसूचना महानिदेशालय
जनरल स्टाफ शाखा, सेना मुख्यालय
डी एच क्यू पी ओ, नई दिल्ली 110 011
Directorate General of Military Intelligence
GS Branch, Army Headquarters
DHQ PO, New Delhi 110 011

12992/RKS/DO *19 Aug 99*

My dear Mr Batra,

1. I am writing this letter to you to tell you how proud we are of your son Capt Vikram. He embodied in himself the best of the Indian Army and its leadership. His raw courage and valour would continue to be remembered for all times to come. I know that his premature loss is irreplaceable and would continue to hurt. I am sure that Vikram inherited his strength of character from you and the family and you will be able to, with God's grace, withstand this tragic loss.

2. We share your grief and are proud of Vikram for his supreme sacrifice and his highly deserved award of Param Vir Chakra. This would ensure that his name gets immortalised in the history of the Nation and would continue to inspire future generations of Indian Army for all times to come. We pray to Almighty to give eternal peace to this great son of India.

With warm regards, Yours sincerely,

Ravi

Shri GL Batra
House No 295
W-5, Palampur
Dist : Kangra (HP)

Phones : 3793438
3019080

ALL INDIA CONGRESS COMMITTEE

24, AKBAR ROAD, NEW DELHI - 110 011

Sonia Gandhi
President

July 30, 1999

Dear Shri Batra,

I was deeply saddened at hearing the tragic news about your son late Capt Vikram Batra. I join the whole country in saluting his valour and his supreme sacrifice.

In this hour of your deep grief, I know only too well how words are of so little consequence. Nevertheless I do want you to know that you and your family are in my thoughts and prayers.

I send you my deepfelt feelings of empathy and support.

Yours sincerely,

Shri Girdhari Lal Batra
F/o Late Capt Vikram Batra
Principal
Sr Secondary School, Paraur
PO Palampur, Dist Kangra
Himachal Pradesh

10, JANPATH, NEW DELHI - 110 011 PH.: 3014481, 3015584

DR. KARAN SINGH

3, NYAYA MARG
CHANAKYAPURI
NEW DELHI -110 021

19 August 1999

My dear Shri Batra,

Your son Major Vikram Batra has been rightly awarded the ***Param Vir Chakra*** for the amazing bravery and patriotism that he displayed in **Operation Vijay** and in which he gave the supreme sacrifice. As former Honorary Colonel of the JAK Regiment, I would like to send you and other members of the family my deep sympathy at your bereavement. Vikram's name will be recorded in glowing letters in the history of the Regiment and the Indian Army as a whole.

When I next visit Kangra, I will personally drop in to call upon you.

With kind regards,

Yours sincerely,

Karan Singh

Shri G.L. Batra
House No. 298, Ward No. 5
Palampur
Dist Kangra
Himachal Pradesh

TEL. : (011) 611-5291 611-1744 FAX : (91-11) 687-3171, 462-7102

PEPSICO INDIA HOLDINGS LIMITED

CHAIRMAN

August 15, 1999

Mr. G.L. Batra
295, W-5, Near Parking Stand
Palampur Dist.
Kangra
Himachal Pradesh – 176061

Dear Mr. Batra,

We are very proud that Captain Bikram Batra has fought against our enemies in Kargil and saved our land from them. I know losing a son is a painful experience, but I am sure you are very proud of your son, as indeed we are.

We are particularly grateful to Captain Batra for having used our Pepsi's well-known slogan "*Dil Maange More*"; he has immortalized this slogan and we owe a lot to him.

If there is anything that we can do for the family we will consider it an honour.

With regards,

Yours sincerely,

PM Sinha

39, DLF CORPORATE PARK, 'S' BLOCK, QUTAB ENCLAVE, PHASE-III, GURGAON - 122 002 (HARYANA) INDIA
TEL. : 91-124-355860 (DIR) PABX 91-124-355860 FAX : 91-124-356281

Prof. P.S. Misra
H.P.E.S. (I) (Retd.)

Ex Director Cum Principal
H.P. University Regional Centre & Govt College
Dy Director Education (North) H.P. Govt

Ekjot Colony, Ramnagar,
DHARAMSALA -176 215
Distt. Kangra (H.P.)
Tel. : (01892) 23030

Dated ....

Dear Shrimati + Shri Batra ji,

We mournfully salute Captain Vikram Batra, your valiant son who has made a history behind him by his gallant bravery at the battle front and supreme sacrifice for the 'Mother Land'. He laid his life so that we may live peace. We pay our homage to martyrs.

We are all with you at this hour and the Nation will ever remember Capt Batra as a 'National Hero'.

It is true that this untimely tragedy is unbearable loss to you and the country but we should feel proud of Capt Batra who has become immortal.

'कैप्टन विक्रम बत्रा अमर रहे !'

May Almighty give you and all of us the courage to bear the unbelievable loss of National Hero and grant peace to Martyr in Heaven.

ओम शान्ति!, शान्ति!, शान्ति !

Sincerely yours,
[signature]

Shri G.L. Batra
Principal
Senior Secondary School
Paraur
Distt Kangra

THE SANDESARA GROUP

STERLING GELATIN

A Division of Sterling Tea & Industries Ltd.
1, Shriniketan Society, Sampatrao Colony, Baroda - 5.
Tel.: (0265) 313331 / 2, 335520, 323917 Fax: (0265) 341099 / 323949
Email : stil.brd@rmg.sprintrpg.ems.vsnl.net.in.

DT: 16TH AUGUST'99

TO,
SHRI GIRDHARILAL BATRA
NR. OLD BUS STATION
PALANPUR
HIMACHAL PRADESH
PINCODE - 176061
TEL.: 01894 32560

Dear Mr. Batra,

I am an Industrialist from Bombay. Though I was not fortunate to meet Vikram personally but during my keen following up of the events in Kargil, I started following up of the various brave acts by Capt. Vikram Batra. I saw him during his interview on Zee TV and Star TV and had developed instant liking for him , for he was a man like that. When one evening in the Ministry of External Affairs briefing, Col.Bikram Singh announced the supreme sacrifice of Capt. Vikram Batra, I was very deeply shocked. When next day I was thinking about Vikram, I could know that I was never so deeply shocked as much except when my mother died in 1989. But to narrate grief would be to undermine the gallantry of Capt. Vikram Batra.

President Kennedy said , it is not important to see what your country gives to you but it is very important to see what you give to your country. Capt. Vikram Batra has written his name at top of the list of the people who give something to the country. The Angels like Vikram never die, they only visit this planet to bless us with their love and sacrifice. Our motherland was fortunate to have son like Vikram and our country has done itself a proud by awarding Paramvir Chakra to Capt. Vikram Batra. They say God's manifestations are many and I am very sure Vikram was one of them.

I have seen you and Vikram's twin brother on television. Please do call me if you are visiting Bombay or western India anytime or otherwise.

With Warm Regards,

NITIN J SANDESARA
CHAIRMAN

Regd. Office : 43, Atlanta Building, Nariman Point, Mumbai - 400 021. Tel. +91 (22) 287 2860 / +91 (22) 284 1229, Fax : +91 (22) 204 1954
Works : ECP Road, Village Karakhadi - 391 210. Ta : Padra, Dist. : Baroda, Gujarat, India. Tel. : (02662) 73292 - 73293 - 73294

SELECT
CITYWALK
Go Shopping!

Respected Mr. Batra,

It is with deep sense of pride as well as with a deep sense of sorrow, I send you this message and compliment you for bringing out a book in honour of your great son Shaheed Capt. Vikram Batra.

Your son lost his life, but gave all of us in India a great sense of pride and secured for the Nation the strategic Kargil Hill. You and your good wife should be proud of your son and it is very thoughtful of you to bring out this book to perpetuate the memory of your brave son. A befitting tribute.

In your hour of remembrance, I, my family and the entire team of Select CITYWALK joins me in paying our respects to your great son and compliments to the wonderful parents who had inculcated in him such high values of devotion and patriotism. Your son is not dead, but he is alive in the hearts of millions of Indians. He is always be a shining star on the horizon of Indian history.

God bless his soul.

With all respects to you and Mrs. Batra,

Yours sincerely,

Inder Sharma
Chairman

Select Infrastructure Pvt. Ltd. (Regd. / Corporate Office) A-3, District Centre, Saket, New Delhi, India 110 017
T +91 11 4211 4211 F +91 11 4211 4222 E contact@selectcitywalk.com W www.selectcitywalk.com
CIN No. U74999DL1979PTC009494

Yeh Dil Maange More

The gun boomed,
Spitting out its deadly shell,
As all around darkness fell.
The hostile peaks seemed menacingly tall,
As you prepared to answer India's call,
Did you swallow your fear,
As you donned your gear,
Did you. curse the moon,
As it lit jour path,
And cheer the clouds,
As they swallowed it up,
Did you stop at each sound,
Fearing that your position had been found,
Did your numb fingers hesitate,
As the enemy you did decimate.

Your courage, your fire they could not confront.
As you lead your men from the front,
Turning their backs the mujahideen fled,
Leaving their posts and their dead.

Post after post, you did get hill
To retake Tiger Hill we were set,
Yet you proclaimed you wanted more,

Unleashing your Jury for an encore,
Till unflinchingly you took the bullets in your chest,
And where you fought, you lay to rest,
Slowly, crimson fumed the virgin snow,
And of your deeds we got to know.

The guns have long been silent,
The monsoons have washed away the pain,
Although things shan't be the same,
The wind will always whistle your tune,
And the valley shall echo your name.

– Anonymous

Homage to Captain Vikram Batra

"Vikram, Vikram," the Kargil ranges called,
"Vikram, Vikram," whispered the soldiers,
Of 13 Jammu and Kashmir Regiment,
As they negotiated the sheer slopes,
With bated breath they clambered
Over the sleet-covered rocks,
Rocks hard and silent since ages,
On whom no human feet, had ever left,
Such immortal footprints of courage.

For the Pakistanis there was left no hope
With "Vikram", the raging volcano
Of matchless valour, none could cope.
Destined was he to become a part of the lore
That would sing the glory of his hero-soul.
On India's TV screens a hundred images flashed,
In which the bravery of Vikram was projected.
" 'Sher Shah', why have you come?" the Pakis taunted,
"To annihilate you I come," our Sher Shah retorted.
To escape from Vikram's fiery onslaught,
To escape from that thundering avalanche,
The enemy drew back and many fell.
On the rocks they lay spread-eagled,

With unseeing eyes, battered, broken and dead,
Thus "Hump", and "Rocky Knob" Vikram's men overran.
Then he was tasked to fly the Tricolour
On well-defended Point 5140 Peak, a difficult feat.
Vikram climbed from behind, he hacked and pulverised,
"Teh Dil Mange More" declared India's pride,
Indians cheered upon hearing his victory cry.
On the captured Pakistani machine-gun he sat astride,
India's Tricolour was unfurled on that peak with pride.
"More" and "More" Vikram asked for, ever more he tried,
Then "More" was he given, asked to conquer Peak 4875,
Where four Pakis with his bare hands he crushed,
The impossible was done, victory almost won,
When to save a wounded comrade, he leaped
From the safety of a bunker, a bullet cleaved
The heart of this lion-king, the Sher Shah, the wonder,
A nation's hope in that time of great danger.

Of his brave mother Kamal Kanta he was the pride,
Of his father Girdhari Lal he was the star child.
Of him, Mother India will forever be proud,
Him the Gods of India will forever bless,
On seventh July, in the year nineteen-ninety-nine
Vikram, of 13 Jammu and Kashmir, laid down his life.

– Shyam Kumari

Braveheart

Here is a tale of a young bravehaart
Who showcased his bravery at the head of India (Kashmir)
An active and brilliant person right from the beginning
A popular figure amongst lot ofpeople
He believed in living life "king-size"
An ardent food and music lover
A Jim-loving person with his friends
He was an obedient son and best brother
A true lover his fiancee was proud of
In his professional life however
He was an achiever, a go-getter
A true son to his motherland
A true gentleman with amazing personality
He cared for others before himself
He was always "fall of life"

Here is the story of this young man
Who faced the enemy with lot of courage and zeal
The outstanding officer in Indian Army
He excelled in every task given to him
A daredevil who was unfa&d by anything
Known as "Sher Shah" in his troup
He had received warning signal from his enemies
"Sher Shah, nobody shall be left to lift your dead bodies,"
To this "Don't worry about us, Pray for your safety" was his reply.

He never feared anything in life
A dedicated officer determined for "total victory"
He had always led his mm to victory
This young lad always volunteered himself for crucial operations
He was passionate about victory and honour
But on one such operation
While battling enemies at the border
He gave tough time to the enemy
*He retaliated every attack with courage and vigour **
He rescued his injured college by saying
"Tu baal bachedaar hai! Hattjaa peeche" and went to face the enemy

But at last he was hit by enemy bullets in his chest
"Jai Mata Di" were his last words
Finally after killing 5 enemies, he succumbed to his injuries
He sacrificed himself for our motherland
India lost its son on July 7, 1999
India still remembers this young hero
This martyr still resides in our heart
And shall live till eternity
He never feared death but embraced it
Salute to this young braveheart
Hero from the beginning, Hero till the end
This was the story of this 24-year-old warrior
A dedicated officer, an exemplary leader, a fighter, a true hero and above all
A selfless human being
India salutes this young officer...
The Param Veer Chakra awarded Kargil Hero...
"Capt. Vikram Batra"
Jai Hind

–Rashmi Kaimal

One of My Gods

Today as I sat praying in the temple of my mind
Ringing the temple bells and showering petals on the gods,
Praying for my life and safety of one and all
Appeared in my mind my god who gave his life,
For the honour and integrity of the nation; worthiest of all
Revered and brave, dear Capt. Vikram Sir, you are the real God
Who fought so gallantly and without fear of none at all,
To finish the demons on the sacred Himalayas of ours!!
The soil that soaked your blood is the heavenly blessed one,
And the river which receives your ashes shall be the holiest of all.
This land, where you were born is indebted to you, dear Sir,
For the supreme sacrifice you made.
For the motherland of ours,
I bow my head on your feet and avow to keep the pledge
You made to save the nation, once and for ever,
Before you became One Of My Gods.

–Pranab Punj

Reference

Chowdhary, Srinjoy, 2000, *Despatches From Kargil,* New Delhi: Penguin Books.

Sawant, Gaurav, 2000, *Dateline Kargil, New Delhi:* Macmillan.

Cardozo, Maj. Gen. lan, 2005, *Param Vir Chakra,* New Delhi: Prabhat Prakashan.

Dutt, Barkha, 2016, *This Unquiet Land, New Delhi:* Aleph Book Company.

Kumari, Shyam, 2006, *Our Heroes: Param Vir Chakra Recipient Series,* Vraja Trust.